MY HEART'S
A SUITCASE

CLARE McINTYRE

Clare McIntyre's *I've been Running* was performed at the Old
Red Lion in May 1986, directed by Terry Johnson. Her second
play, *Low Level Panic*, which was commissioned and presented by
the Women's Playhouse Trust, was first performed at the Royal
Court Theatre Upstairs in February 1988, directed by Nancy
Meckler, and this production was subsequently revived at the
Lyric Theatre Hammersmith in the summer of 1989. *Low Level
Panic* also won her the Samuel Beckett Theatre Award for 1989.
Clare McIntyre has an extensive career as an actress in theatre,
film and television.

by the same author

Low Level Panic

CLARE McINTYRE

My Heart's A Suitcase

A Royal Court Programme/Text published by

NICK HERN BOOKS

A division of Walker Books Limited

A Nick Hern Book

My Heart's a Suitcase first published in 1990 as an original
paperback by Nick Hern Books, a division of Walker Books
Limited, 87 Vauxhall Walk, London SE11 5HJ

My Heart's a Suitcase copyright © 1990 by Clare McIntyre
Front cover illustration: Photo copyright © 1990 by
Lesley McIntyre. Reproduced with permission.

Set in ITC New Baskerville and printed in Great Britain by
Expression Printers Limited, London N7 9DP

British Library Cataloguing in Publication Data

McIntyre, Clare
    My heart's a suitcase.
    I. Title
    822.914

ISBN 1-85459-072-3

Caution
All rights whatsoever in this play are strictly reserved. Requests
to reproduce the text in whole or in part should be addressed to
the publisher. Application for performance in any medium or
for translation into any language should be addressed to the
author's sole agent, Curtis Brown Ltd, 162-168 Regent Street,
London W1R 5TB.

A BRIEF HISTORY OF
THE ENGLISH
STAGE COMPANY
AT THE
ROYAL COURT

The English Stage Company was formed in 1956 to bring serious writing back to the stage. The aim was that writers should explore subjects drawn from contemporary life and that the plays produced would be challenging and innovatory as well as of the highest quality. With only the second production the company struck gold: John Osborne's *LOOK BACK IN ANGER* is the play that has been credited with propelling British theatre into the modern age. Since then, the English Stage Company has never looked back. As well as reviving often neglected classics, it has premiered the work of playwrights who are now performed the world over, attracting such stars as Olivier, Richardson, Gielgud and Ashcroft into new plays by writers such as John Osborne, David Storey, Edward Bond, Arnold Wesker and Ann Jellicoe.

The line continued with writers such as David Hare and Howard Brenton. Both were first produced at the Royal Court early on in their careers. More recently, Caryl Churchill has reached a wide audience after early beginnings in the Theatre Upstairs and writers such as Timberlake Wertenbaker, Hanif Kureishi, Jim Cartwright and Anne Devlin have had work produced. Recent critical and box office successes have included *TOP GIRLS, SERIOUS MONEY, ROAD, TOM AND VIV, INSIGNIFICANCE* and *OUR COUNTRY'S GOOD.*

After thirty-three years, the Royal Court Theatre is still the most important forum in Britain for the production of new work. Scores of plays first seen in Sloane Square have become part of the national and international dramatic repertoire. It is now the only theatre with a main stage that has new work continually in production and, although funding shortages mean that it can only function on an occasional basis, the Theatre Upstairs remains one of the most significant studio theatres in the country.

As a place where reputations are made, and as a bridgehead to other areas of the profession and to film and television, the Royal Court's contribution to British Theatre is incalculable.

THE ROYAL COURT THEATRE
presents

MY HEART'S A SUITCASE
by Clare McIntyre

CHRIS	**Frances Barber**
LUGGAGE	**Amelda Brown**
HANNAH	**Sylvestra le Touzel**
TUNIS	**Anna Patrick**
ELLIOT	**Fred Pearson**
PEST	**Paul Wyett**

The play is set in Brighton

There will be one interval of fifteen minutes

Directed by	**Max Stafford-Clark**
Designed by	**Anabel Temple**
Lighting by	**Steve Whitson**
Sound by	**Bryan Bowen**
Costume Supervisors	**Jennifer Cook** and **Katie Birrell**
Assistant Director	**Anna Birch**
Stage Manager	**Gemma Bodley**
Deputy Stage Manager	**Katie Spencer**
Assistant Stage Manager	**Ali Carron**
Student Assistant Stage Managers	**Douglas Turnbull** and **Alex Wheeler**

Wardrobe care by PERSIL and COMFORT. Adhesive by COPYDEX and EVODE LTD. Ioniser for the lighting control room by THE LONDON IONISER CENTRE (836 0211). Cordless drill by MAKITA ELECTRIC (UK) LTD. Watches by THE TIMEX CORPORATION. Batteries by EVER READY. Refrigerators by ELECTROLUX and PHILIPS MAJOR APPLIANCES LTD. Microwave by TOSHIBA UK LTD. Kettles for rehearsals by MORPHY RICHARDS. Video for casting purposes by HITACHI. Coffee machines by CONA. Microwave for backstage use kindly supplied by ZANUSSI LTD. Freezer for backstage use supplied by ELECTROLUX "Now that's a good idea".

Funded by

LONDON BOROUGHS GRANTS SCHEME

FUNDED BY THE ROYAL
BOROUGH OF KENSINGTON
AND CHELSEA

Arts Council Funded

BIOGRAPHIES

FRANCES BARBER - Theatre includes: *Oooh La La* (Hull Truck); *Hard Feelings, Turning Over* (Bush); *Summer and Smoke* (Leicester Haymarket); *Camille, Hamlet, Love's Labour's Lost, The Dead Monkey* (RSC); *Macbeth* (Royal Exchange), *Twelfth Night* (Renaissance). TV includes: *Annie Besant, The Storyteller, Hard Feelings, Behaving Badly, The Nightmare Years, Home Sweet Home, The Grasscutter, Twelfth Night, Clem*. Films include: *A Zed and Two Noughts, Prick Up Your Ears, Castaway, Acceptable Levels, Sammy and Rosie Get Laid, We Think the World Of You, Duck, Chambre-a-part*.

AMELDA BROWN - Theatre includes: *Apart From George* (National Theatre tour and Royal Court), *Macbeth* (National Theatre tour); *A Midsummer Night's Dream, The Real Thing, Village Wooing, The Lane* (Birmingham); *Fen* (Joint Stock tour and at the Royal Court), *Fire in the Park* (Joint Stock tour), *A Mouthful of Birds* (Joint Stock tour and at the Royal Court), *Power of the Dog* (Joint Stock tour); *Falkland Sound* and *Child's Play* (Coventry); *Trafford Tanzi* (Bolton); *Top Girls* (Leicester); *Girl Talk* (Soho Poly). TV includes: *The Rainbow, The Practice and Sherlock Holmes*. Films: *Spirit, Hope and Glory, Little Dorritt, An English Christmas* and *Biddy*.

SYLVESTRA LE TOUZEL - For the Royal Court: *Glasshouses, Ourselves Alone* and *Unity*. Other theatre includes: *Hamlet* (RSC tour); *Countrymania* and *The Wandering Jew* (National); *Dracula* (Lyric); *The Alchemist* and *The London Cuckolds* (Lyric Hammersmith), *The Fall* and *The War at Home* (Hampstead); *The Understanding* (Strand); *Faery Queen* (Aix-en-Provence); *Strange Fruit* (Sheffield); *Harvest* (Ambassadors); *The Crucible* (Birmingham). TV includes: *Naming the Names, Seeing in the Dark, The Dog it was that Died, Making Out, A Vote for Hitler, Mansfield Park, Crimes, Donal and Sally, This Year Next Year, Family Affair, L.S. Lowry, A Private View*. Film: *Short and Curlies*.

ANNA PATRICK - Theatre includes: *The Winter's Tale, Macbeth, Sarcophagus, The Storm, Worlds Apart, Great White Hope* (RSC); *Othello* and *A Child's Christmas in Wales* (Theatre Clywd); *The Duchess of Malfi* (Duke of Cambridge); *Mad Woman of Chaillot* (Lilian Bayliss); *Lady Windermere's Fan* (Citizens, Glasgow); *A Midsummer Night's Dream, Talking With* (Everyman); *Orphan* (Greenwich). TV: *South of the Border* and *Sixth Sense*.

FRED PEARSON - For the Royal Court: *The Winter Dancers, The Good Woman of Sichuan, Three More Sleepless Nights, Tibetan Inroads.* Other theatre includes: *A Fair Quarrel, Guys And Dolls, The Government Inspector, Pravda, The Futurists, King Lear* (National Theatre); *Our Friends in the North, Clay, The Winter's Tale* (RSC, Barbican), *Much Ado About Nothing* and *The Caucasian Chalk Circle* (RSC Tour); *The Ragged Trousered Philanthropists, The Crimes of the Vautrin* (Joint Stock); *The Father* (Greenwich); *The Relapse* (Lyric, Hammersmith); *The Plough and the Stars* (Exchange, Manchester); *Death of a Salesman* (Theatre Royal, York); *Heartbreak House* (Shared Experience). TV includes: *Pasmore, Clapperclaw, Tales Out of School, Coronation Street, The Bill, Scoop, A Bit of a Do.*

ANABEL TEMPLE (Designer) - For the Royal Court: *Rock in Water, Ambulance, The Royal Borough, Built on Sand* and *Inventing a New Colour* (co-production with Bristol Old Vic). Other theatre includes: *In the Ruins* (Bristol Old Vic); *Women on Men* (Opera Factory\London Sinfonietta).

STEVE WHITSON (Lighting Designer) - For the Royal Court: *Sleeping Nightie.* Other theatre includes: *Macbeth* (Odyssey Theatre); *The Bastille Dances* (Station House Opera at the National). He has also done premiere lights for works by Andy Warhol, Sam Shepard, Rose English, Edward Bond, David Lan and Caryl Churchill. He is also a film director and script-writer.

PAUL WYETT - Theatre includes: *Space* (Soho Poly); *Salt of the Earth* (Nottingham). TV includes: *First of the Summer Wine, Hang Gliding. Film: A Soldier's Tale* and *Hothouse.*

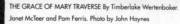

WOMEN WRITERS
AT THE COURT 1956 to 1990

In 1956 John Osborne's LOOK BACK IN ANGER took the
British Theatre by storm and the era of the angry young
man had begun. But, sadly, as is often the case, the angry
young women had to wait in the wings before finding a
platform for their voice. And perhaps it is only now, 35
years on, that one can say with any measure of confidence
that women writers are arriving in numbers. A brief look at
some statistics bears out this statement.

From 1956 to 1980, the English Stage Company produced,
either on the Royal Court's Main Stage, in the Theatre
Upstairs or as one of the influential Sunday Night "Plays
without Decor", 475 different plays. Of these 39 (8%) were
written or co-written by a woman and a third of these were
by two women, Ann Jellicoe and Caryl Churchill.   From
1980 to the end of 1989, 180 plays were presented at the
Royal Court, of which 53 (29%) were written or co-written
by women. From 1985 to Spring 1990, 9 of the 34 plays
presented on the Main Stage will have been by women:
three by Caryl Churchill, two by Timberlake Wertenbaker
and one each by Anne Devlin, Charlotte Keatley, Sarah
Daniels and Clare McIntyre. Over the same period a rather
higher proportion of the work in the Theatre Upstairs was
by women: 11 out of 25 productions and 30 of the
rehearsed readings (the cheap contemporary alternative to
the more fully rehearsed "Plays without Decor"). 25% of the
unsolicited scripts received through the post are by women,
and the Young Writers' Festival has consistently both
received and produced twice as much work by young
women. As for the future, 5 of the 14 current Main Stage
commissions are with women writers and 7 of the 14
commissions for the Theatre Upstairs. To an extent, these
figures are shared by other new London writing theatres.
Over the last 9 years 23% of the Bush's output has been by
women, but this percentage has risen to 40% over the last 3
years. On the other hand, neither Hampstead nor the
National nor the RSC have accumulated any body of work
by women.

So, clearly there is a steadily growing body of women's
writing being presented at the Royal Court and elsewhere
though it is still to be measured as much in terms of
potential as achievement. The bulk of women's writing is still
presented as either rehearsed readings or in studio theatres.
This means the announcement of a 17% increase for the
Royal Court, which will enable the Theatre Upstairs to re-
open, is of major importance to a new generation of female
writers.

In the early days of the English Stage Company, the only
woman to be accepted by the prestigious Writers' Group
was Ann Jellicoe, whose reputation had been established by
THE SPORT OF MY MAD MOTHER and THE KNACK. Her
memory of that period makes it clear that the attempt to find

and involve women in theatre writing was not a priority. *"I felt I'd done something remarkable, being a woman who'd got through....at the same time, I didn't appreciate what tremendous disadvantages I was working under....the men didn't really take a woman seriously."* Nevertheless, Ann Jellicoe went on to have a number of plays produced at the Court and did pioneering work with the Young People's Theatre. Even so, until the advent of Caryl Churchill, who had her first play produced in the early '70's, no other woman was strongly affiliated to the Royal Court. Of course, a few women had had their plays produced - Shelagh Delaney was successful with *THE LION IN LOVE* in 1960, and Adrienne Kennedy made it to the Theatre Upstairs in 1968. Some women in the 70's were even produced on the Main Stage. There was Marguerite Duras with *THE LOVERS OF VIORNE* in 1971, Edna O'Brien with *A PAGAN PLACE* in 1972 and Mary O'Malley with her hugely successful play *ONCE A CATHOLIC* in 1977. But there was no permanent association with the theatre for any of these writers.

Caryl Churchill's work at the Royal Court began with the production of *OWNERS* in 1972 and has continued with 11 of her subsequent plays being seen at the Court. Her plays of the 1980's have been among the most popular in the Royal Court's history, including her most recent success *ICECREAM* (in 1989), but, before that, several of her plays were produced in the Theatre Upstairs. These were more experimental and clearly show the importance of allowing a writer time to find her own voice and style. The end of the 1970's and the new decade saw the popularisation of the women's movement with growing pressure for women to be represented in all areas of public life and, subsequently, in that most public of art forms, the theatre. The new women's companies continued to unearth more writers and the increased political awareness of many women working in the theatre led to the formation of pressure groups such as Women in Entertainment and to the staging of special events such as Women Live in 1982. Gradually theatres began to take some notice and, at the Court, the decade got into its stride with Caryl Churchill's seminal and visionary play *TOP GIRLS* in 1982. This was followed by Sarah Daniels' play *MASTERPIECES*, which made a lasting impact in 1983, proving that fierce, polemic and uncompromising feminism does not necessarily lead to low box office returns. Indeed, the commercial record of women writers has always been good; possibly because a large proportion of all theatre-goers are female, indeed surveys have shown they form a majority of the Royal Court's audience, and also because plays by women have expressed some of contemporary society's most urgent concerns.

Other plays by women on the Main Stage in the 1980's have included Andrea Dunbar's remarkable piece *THE ARBOR* (1980) written when she was only 16; Sue Townsend's *THE GREAT CELESTIAL COW*, produced by Joint Stock, and, last year, Charlotte Keatley's lively and popular *MY MOTHER SAID I NEVER SHOULD*. Timberlake Wertenbaker, another woman writer now closely associated with the Court, made her Main Stage debut in 1985 with her remarkable play *THE GRACE OF MARY TRAVERSE*. Her most recent play, *OUR COUNTRY'S GOOD* (1989), has, along with Caryl Churchill's *SERIOUS MONEY* (1987), been one of the most influential Royal Court hits of the decade. Last year it was produced in the West End and toured world-wide.

At the start of the 1990's things look good for women at the Royal Court. The Theatre Upstairs is shortly to be used for a workshop on Kay Adshead's ambitious new play, *BACILLUS*. While, on the Main Stage in the spring, the Women's Playhouse Trust (a company that has been a major force in bringing forward new women playwrights) will be co-producing Sarah Daniels' latest play *BESIDE HERSELF*. Indeed it was the Women's Playhouse Trust (in association with the Royal Court) that produced Clare McIntyre's first play, *LOW LEVEL PANIC*, in the Theatre Upstairs in 1987. But the best thing of all is that a new decade is beginning with a fresh name on the Main Stage of the Royal Court - and that name is a woman's. I hope there will be many more such breakthroughs as the nineties progress.

In conclusion, it is worth noting that, at the beginning of 1989, it was remarked that the Royal Court was in the midst of presenting an unbroken run of six different plays by women, (Timberlake Wertenbaker's *OUR COUNTRY'S GOOD*, Caryl Churchill's *ICECREAM* and Charlotte Keatley's *MY MOTHER SAID I NEVER SHOULD* Downstairs; and in the Theatre Upstairs, *A HERO'S WELCOME* and *A ROCK IN WATER* by Winsome Pinnock together with the original reading of *MY HEART'S A SUITCASE*.) It was suggested that something be made of this - a joint interview with all the writers perhaps? However, the writers themselves resisted the idea, one argued firmly against it. Clearly, women in the theatre no longer believe they should be treated as an anomaly. They feel they have arrived and are here to stay. Let's hope so.

Kate Harwood January 1990

COMING NEXT
01-730 1745/2254

MAIN HOUSE
From 29 March
The WPT and the Royal Court Theatre present
BESIDE HERSELF
by Sarah Daniels
Directed by Jules Wright

BESIDE HERSELF continues in the tradition of Sarah Daniels' best work. It is a challenging no-holds-barred look at major themes, preoccupations and principles that have emerged in Britain over the past ten years.

Sunday 22 April
SOTHEBY'S AT THE ROYAL COURT

In aid of the Olivier Appeal for the Royal Court Theatre, Sotheby's are holding a charity auction of theatrical memorabilia and works of art connected to people "in the business".

From 11th May
The Royal Court Theatre presents the Bristol Old Vic's production of
IN THE RUINS
by Nick Dear
Directed by Paul Unwin

The time is 1817. The King, George III, is 77 years old and quite, quite barmy. Nick Dear's play looks back on the astonishing events of George's long reign and provides a history lesson which is surprisingly topical.

"Patrick Malahide's performance is masterly" The Guardian

Also:
GARRICK THEATRE
Charing Cross Road, London WC2
Diana Bliss and Frank & WoJi Gero present
The Royal Court Theatre's production of
OUR COUNTRY'S GOOD
by Timberlake Wertenbaker
based on Thomas Keneally's novel 'The Playmaker'

Directed by Max Stafford-Clark

Tickets available from the Royal Court Theatre

THE OLIVIER APPEAL

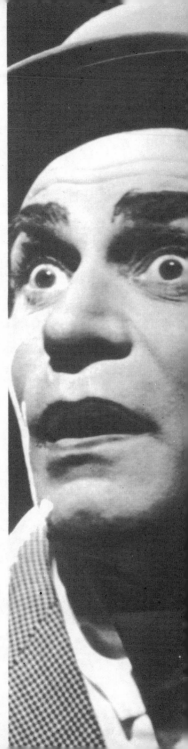

The Royal Court Theatre was very proud of
Lord Olivier's patronage of our Appeal. It
will continue in his name as a memorial to
his life and talent. The Appeal was launched
in June 1988 - the Royal Court's 100th
anniversary year. The target is £800,000 to
repair and refurbish the theatre and to
enable the English Stage Company to
maintain and continue its worldwide
reputation as Britain's "National Theatre of
new writing". The Royal Court would like to
thank the following for their generous
contributions to the Appeal:

Laurence Olivier 1907-1989 (Snowdon)

THE ROYAL COURT THEATRE SOCIETY

For many years now Members of the Royal Court Theatre Society have received special notice of new productions, but why not become a Friend, Associate or a Patron of the Royal Court, thereby involving yourself directly in maintaining the high standard and unique quality of Royal Court productions - while enjoying complimentary tickets to the shows themselves?

Subscriptions run for one year; to become a Friend £60 (joint), £40 (single), an Associate £400, a Patron £1,000.
(membership costs £12)

PATRONS Jeffrey Archer, Diana Bliss, Caryl Churchill, Issac Davidov, Alfred Davis, Mr & Mrs Nicholas Egon, Mrs Henny Gestetner, Lady Eileen Joseph, Henry Kaye, Stonewall Productions Ltd. Tracey Ullman, Julian Wadham, Timberlake Wertenbaker, Irene Worth.

ASSOCIATES Peter Boizot, David Capelli, Michael Codron, Jeremy Conway, Stephen Fry, Elizabeth Garvie, The Earl of Gowrie, David Hart, London Arts Discovery Tours, Patricia Marmont, Barbara Minto, Greville Poke, Michael Serlin, Sir Dermot de Trafford, Nick Hern Books, Richard Wilson.

FRIENDS Paul Adams, S.M.Alexander, Roger Allam & Susan Todd, Robin Anderson, Jane Annakin, John Arthur, Francis & Cherry Baden-Powell, Mrs M.Bagust, Martine Baker, Veronica Ball, Dee Barnfield, Linda Bassett, Paul Bater, Richard Baylis, Josephine Beddoe, Laura Birkett, Anthony Blond, Bob Boas, Brian Boylan, Irving H.Brecker, Katie Bradford, Jim Broadbent, Alan Brodie, Ralph Brown, A.J.H.Buckley, Stuart Burge, Kevin Byrne, Neil Goodhue Cady, Laurence Cann, Susan Card, Annie Castledine, Ben Chamberlain, Guy Chapman, Steve Childs, Ruby Cohn, Angela Coles, Lee Collier, Sandra Cook, Lynn & Bernard Cottrell, Lou Coulson, Peter Cregeen, Harriet Cruickshank, B.R.Cuzner, I.Dallaway, Mrs Der Pao Graham, Anne Devlin, Mrs V.A.Dimant, Cathy Dodgeon, Julia Dos Santos, R.H. & B.H.Dowler, Adrian Charles Dunbar, Susan Dunnett, Pamela Edwardes, George A.Elliott III, Gillian Emmett, Patricia England, Jan Evans, Trevor Eve, Kenneth Ewing, Kate Feast, Leonard Fenton, Mr & Mrs Thomas Fenton, M.H.Flash, Robert Fox, Gilly Fraser, Dr Robert Galvin, David Gant, Kerry Gardner, Sarah Garner, Anne Garwood, Alfred Molina & Jill Gascoine, Timothy Gee, B.H. Geismar, Jonathan Gems, Frank & Woji Gero, Ronald Gidseg, Beth Goddard, Lord Goodman, A.C.Gorva, Roger Graef, Joan Grahame, Rod Hall, Lorraine Hamilton, Sharon Hamper, Shahab Hanif, Rosemary Hanson, J.H.Hards, A.M.Harrison, Vivien Heilbron, Jan Harvey, Peter Headill, Sarah Hellings, Jocelyn Herbert, Ashley & Pauline Hill, Angus Hone, David Horovitch, Jack Howard, Susan J.Hoyle, Nigel P.Hudson, Dusty Hughes, Vi Hughes, Diana Hull, Susan Imhof, Trevor Ingman, Kenny Ireland, Jonathan Issacs, Alison E.Jackson, Richard Jackson, Dick Jarrett, B.E.Jenkins, Hugh Jenkins, Dominic Jephcott, Paul Jesson, Rowland Jobson, Donald Jones, Dr & Mrs David Josefowitz, Andrew Joseph, Annely Juda, Elizabeth Karr Tashman, Sharon Kean, Alice Kennelly, Jean Knox, Mark Knox, Mrs O.Lahr, Duncan Lamb, Dr R.J.Lande, Iain Lanyon, Hugh Laurie, Peter Leadill, Alison Leathart, Peter Ledeboer, C.C.Lee, Sheila Lemon, Peter L.Levy, Tony and Julia Ling, Robert S.Linton, Mr & Mrs M.M.Littman, Roger & Moira Lubbock, John & Erica Macdonald, Mr & Mrs Roger Mace, Suzie Mackenzie, Dr Anne Mackie, Marina Mahler, Paul Mari, Pete Maric, Nick Marston, Marina Martin, Patricia Marx, Anna Massey, S.A.Mason, Paul Matthews, Elaine Maycock, Philip L.McDonald, Ian McMillan, James Midgley, Louise Miller, Anthony Minghella, L.A.G.Morris, Mimi Morris, Mr G. F.Mulhern, T. Murnaghan, Alex Nash, Rosy Nasreen & Dr Conal Liam Mannion, Linda Newns, Sally Newton, John Nicholls, Michael Nyman, Richard O'Brien, Eileen & John O'Keefe, Donald O'Leary, Elizabeth and Paul O'Shea, Stephen Oliver, Gary Olsen, Mark Padmore, Norman Papp, Alan David & Jane Penrose, Pamela Percy, Ronald Pickup, Pauline Pinder, Harold Pinter, Nigel Planer, Laura Plumb, Peter Polkinghorne, Adam Pollock, Dr A.G.Poulsen Hansen, Trevor Preston, Dr G.Pullen and Mrs P.Black, R.Puttick, Margaret Ramsay, Jane Rayne, Alex Renton, B.J. & Rosmarie Reynolds, E.W.Richards, Alan Rickman, David Robb, Martin & Jennifer Roddy, R.S.Rubin, Christie Ryan, Jeremy and Nora Sayers, George Schneider, Leah Schmidt, Julia Scott, Rosemary Squire, Martin & Glynis Scurr, Jennifer Sebag-Montefiore, Mrs L.M.Sieff, Paul Sinclair Brooke, Andrew Sinclair and Sonia Melchett, Ms A.M.Jamieson & Mr A.P.Smith, Peter A.Smith, Jane Snowden, Sir Kerry and Lady St.Johnston, Max Stafford-Clark, Ms Caroline Staunton, Louise Stein, Jenny Stein, Jeff Steitzer, Lindsay Stevens, Pearl Stewart, Richard Stokes, Richard Stone, Geoffrey Strachan, Rob Sutherland, Dudley Sutton, K & A Sydow, Audrey & Gordon Taylor, Steve Tedbury, Nigel Terry, Mary Trevelyan, Amanda and R.L.W.Triggs, Elizabeth Troop, Mrs Anne Underwood, Kiomars Vejdani, Maureen Vincent, Karen and Wes Wadman, Andrew Wadsworth, Harriet Walter, Julie Walters, Tim Watson, Nicholas Wright, Charles and Victoria Wright, Peter B.Young.

FOR THE ROYAL COURT

DIRECTION

Artistic Director	**Max Stafford-Clark**
Casting Director	**Lisa Makin**
Acting Literary Manager	**Melanie Kenyon**
Assistant Director	**Philip Howard**
Artistic Assistant	**Helen Carter**
Arts Council Writer in Residence	**Clare McIntyre**
Thames Television Writer in Residence	**Victoria Hardie**
Gerald Chapman Award Trainee Director	**Anna Birch**

PRODUCTION

Production Manager	**Bo Barton**
Chief Electrician	**Johanna Town**
Acting Chief Electrician	**James Armstrong**
Acting Deputy Chief Electrician	**Denis O'Hare**
Sound Designer	**Bryan Bowen**
Board Operator	**Jonquil Pantin***
Master Carpenter	**Chris Bagust**
Acting Deputy Master Carpenter	**Matthew Smith**
Wardrobe Supervisor	**Jennifer Cook**
Deputy Wardrobe Supervisor	**Cathie Skilbeck**
Wardrobe Assistant	**Catherine Berrinbaume**

ADMINISTRATION

General Manager	**Graham Cowley**
Assistant to General Manager	**Georgia Cheales**
Finance Administrator	**Mark Rubinstein**
Finance Assistant	**Rachel Harrison**
Press (730 2652)	**Tamsin Thomas**
Marketing and Publicity Manager	**Guy Chapman**
Development Manager	**Anne-Marie Thompson**
Development Assistant	**Sue Wilson**
House Manager	**Gambol Parker**
Deputy House Manager	**Alison Smith**
Bookshop	**Angela Toulmin-Hunt***
Box Office Manager	**Gill Russell**
Box Office Assistants	**Gerald Brooking, Rita Sharma**
Stage Door/Telephonists	**Angela Toulmin-Hunt*, Jan Noyce***
Evening Stage Door	**Tyrone Lucas***
Maintenance	**John Lorrigio***
Cleaners	**Eileen Chapman*, Ivy Jones***
Firemen	**Paul Kleinmann*, David Wyatt***

YOUNG PEOPLE'S THEATRE

Director	**Elyse Dodgson**
Administrator	**Dominic Tickell**
Youth and Community Worker	**Euton Daley**

* Part-time staff

COUNCIL:

Chairman: Matthew Evans, Chris Bagust, Bo Barton, Stuart Burge, Anthony C.Burton, Brian Cox, Harriet Cruickshank, Simon Curtis, Allan Davis, David Lloyd Davis, Robert Fox, Jocelyn Herbert, Hanif Kureishi, Sonia Melchett, James Midgley, Joan Plowright CBE, Greville Poke, Richard Pulford, Jane Rayne, Jim Tanner, Sir Hugh Willatt.

This theatre is associated with the Regional Theatre Young Directors' Scheme and with the Thames Television Theatre Writers' Scheme

MY HEART'S
A SUITCASE

My Heart's a Suitcase was first staged at the Royal Court Theatre in London. First preview was 8 February 1990; press night was 13 February 1990.

Characters
CHRIS, thirty
HANNAH, thirty
TUNIS, early twenties
LUGGAGE, indeterminate age
ELLIOTT, early fifties
PEST, eighteen

The Set: The setting for the play is a room in a flat on the first floor of a building overlooking the sea in Brighton. The building is at least a hundred years old. It was built in the heyday of the English Riviera when the Front was promenaded by the wealthy rather than the unemployed. The room has a pair of large windows which overlook the sea. They have been left open. Torn, semi-drawn net curtains are blowing in the breeze. There are autumn leaves on the floor. There is a cupboard on one wall. Among the things in the room there needs to be a television: this is standing on a little table and is covered by a dust sheet. There also needs to be a telephone and a sofa. There are two doors into the room: one, the front door as it were into the flat, the other a door leading to the rest of the flat. In the text I refer to the former as the front or exterior door and the latter as the interior door.

The set, like the play, should be both real and unreal. Two of the characters come and go through the walls.

Scene One

Friday afternoon 4 p.m.

CHRIS *and* HANNAH *are standing in the room. The exterior door is open. They have 'overnight' bags with them.* CHRIS*'s is a plastic laundry bag.* HANNAH*'s is a rucksack.*

CHRIS. I don't like it.

HANNAH. It's wonderful. God it's amazing . . . It's enormous.

CHRIS. I don't like it.

HANNAH. Why?

CHRIS. I just don't.

HANNAH. Why?

CHRIS. It gives me the creeps.

HANNAH. Why?

CHRIS. Stop saying 'Why' will you.

HANNAH. What's the matter?

CHRIS. Let's go and stay in a hotel. It's bloody derelict.

HANNAH. It's not. It's just been empty for a while that's all.

CHRIS. The whole building's empty. There's no one in the flat downstairs is there?

HANNAH. I don't know.

CHRIS. There isn't. I looked.

HANNAH. Well they're new flats aren't they? It's brilliant. You can see the sea. Who lives in places like this? Retired colonels?

CHRIS. People who've got au pairs.

HANNAH. I wonder if you can see France.

CHRIS. 'Course you can't. Let's go to a hotel.

HANNAH. I can't afford a hotel.

CHRIS. I'll pay.

HANNAH. You haven't got any money.

CHRIS. It's only for the weekend. We'll find somewhere.

HANNAH. I thought this Colin bloke wanted you to use the place.

CHRIS. He does.

HANNAH. Well then. Don't look a gift-horse in the mouth.

CHRIS. What's that supposed to mean?

HANNAH. Why are you in such a pissy mood? It's brilliant here. It's a bit weird but I really like it. You're not going to stay here on your own are you?

CHRIS. No.

HANNAH. So what are you getting in a flap about? It was your idea to come. You invited me. Remember? Colin's your friend not mine.

CHRIS. I'll pay for a hotel.

HANNAH. You can't afford a hotel and neither can I and I like it here. You've brought your sleeping bag haven't you? We could make a fire and . . .

CHRIS. Where? There's no fireplace.

HANNAH. I'm not going to drive all the way back until I've had my weekend away.

CHRIS. I'm not saying we should go back.

HANNAH. I'd rather go back than waste money on a hotel.

CHRIS. Alright, let's go back.

HANNAH. Don't talk wet. What'd you say to Colin? He'd think you were barmy.

CHRIS. There's been a dosser in here. You can smell him.

HANNAH. I can't.

CHRIS. I'm going to tell Colin we got here too late and his holiday flat's been squatted by a bunch of winos.

HANNAH. Is that why he wants us to stay here? To stop it being squatted?

CHRIS. I wouldn't put it past him.

HANNAH. What a laugh.

CHRIS. Believe me I know him. That's the way his mind works . . . He wasn't lying when he said there wasn't anything here was he?

HANNAH. Has he just bought it?

CHRIS. Must have done. I really don't know.

HANNAH. He has to have money to burn to have this place and a home as well.

CHRIS. He has.

HANNAH. It's another world money isn't it? I suppose it's an investment.

CHRIS. Knowing Colin it will be. Or it'll be tax deductible. Or it'll be in his wife's name and it'll be a fiddle. Or the company had to lose some money and it'll just sit here, empty, increasing in value till they sell it. Whatever it is it'll be about making a killing, that's for sure.

HANNAH. Who cares?

CHRIS. Feels like that window's been open for centuries. Feels like the whole place has been left here to rot.

HANNAH. 'S a good job somebody's bought it then isn't it? I thought we were going to play at being rich for the weekend. I don't want to stay in a poxy little hotel. Knowing you we'd end up in a grotty bed and breakfast and they'd want us out by dawn and we'd spend the whole weekend killing time with nowhere to go. You've been invited to stay here for the weekend . . .

CHRIS. As long as I like.

HANNAH. Well then that's settled. Whether it's a tax dodge or an investment or a red herring or a white elephant doesn't matter a monkey's to me.

CHRIS. At least bed and breakfasts aren't creepy: they've got signs of life about them like other people and carpets and curtains.

HANNAH. You hate other people.

She exits through the interior door. CHRIS *removes a dust sheet and uncovers a television on a small table. She switches the television on. At this stage the volume is turned right down. She channel-dodges.*

HANNAH (*off*). Jesus! Get a load of the bathroom. It's got double wash hand basins. You can shave together . . . Gold taps . . . Talk about gross.

CHRIS *turns up the television.*

Have you got a television in there?

CHRIS. Yeah.

She listens to the following news report. (HANNAH's speech and the sound from the television should overlap it. The overlap is marked **).

TELEVISION. The body of fourteen year old Tracy Hodge, the girl who disappeared six days ago while on her morning paper round, has been found in a shallow grave in woods only five hundred yards from her home. She had been sexually assaulted and strangled. Police, trying to piece together Tracy's last movements, believe she may have been alerted to her danger and was attempting to get home when she was abducted.** Her bicycle was found in a bus shelter close to her home and not on her paper route. They suspect the murderer may have alarmed her and then followed her as she tried to get home, abducted her in a car and then returned days later with her body and left it in the woods. Tracy's parents, who have no other children, are staying with friends. They were unavailable for comment. There is a police help-line for anyone who feels they may have information: it is 041 . . .

CHRIS *turns the television off.*

HANNAH (*off*). **There's another one in here. How decadent can you get? Bloody Hell, you can change channels from the bed. I think we should move in, be caretakers. (*She switches the television on. We can hear it faintly.*)

CHRIS. **What?

HANNAH (*off*). **We could be caretakers. We could swan around all day watching telly and getting paid for it. That'd beat working wouldn't it?

HANNAH *enters.*

CHRIS. Let's go.

HANNAH. What's got into you? We've just taken three hours getting here. Why can't you relax?

CHRIS. I don't know.

HANNAH. Listen.

CHRIS. What?

Pause.

HANNAH. Absolute quiet.

From the sofa CHRIS *removes a lumpy object which is beginning to irritate her. It is a man's jacket.*

CHRIS. There has been a dosser here. He's left his jacket.

HANNAH. It won't be a dosser's: it'll be one of the workmen's.

CHRIS. It's filthy. We can't stay here if . . .

HANNAH. Yes we can and we're going to. It could be anyone's jacket. And if it is a dosser's . . . well . . . he isn't here now is he?

CHRIS. What are we going to do here all weekend. There's nothing here.

HANNAH. Don't be so pathetic. There's masses to do.

CHRIS. What?

HANNAH. I don't know. You can always find something.

CHRIS. Do you know what this place reminds me of?

HANNAH. What?

CHRIS. My life.

HANNAH. Oh, for Heaven's sake.

CHRIS. It does.

HANNAH. Brilliant.

CHRIS. No, I was just wondering why . . .

HANNAH. Well don't.

CHRIS. No I mean . . .

HANNAH (*interrupts*). Why wonder? Why worry? Stop thinking. You're on holiday. Right?

She exits through the interior door. PEST *walks through a wall. He is carrying an air pistol. He wears light blue jeans, a shirt and trainers.*

PEST *is a bad memory, who inhabits* CHRIS's *imagination.*

PEST. Lady.

CHRIS (*she starts and turns to confront him*). No. Not now. This is my weekend away. I'm here to clear my head.

HANNAH (*off*). What are we going to do for food?

CHRIS *turns towards the interior door.* PEST *exits.*

HANNAH. Chris?

CHRIS. I don't know.

HANNAH (*off*). What do you feel like?

Blackout.

Scene Two

Friday midnight.

CHRIS *is drinking whisky.* HANNAH *is lying spreadeagled on her back. Her glass of whisky beside her. They have had a take-away and the debris is on the floor. The light in the room is partly from the street lights outside, yellow light coming through the bare windows, and partly from the lights in the room. These should be soft and bearable, not naked, overhead light bulbs.* HANNAH *remains completely immobile until indicated in the script. She has changed her trousers.*

CHRIS. When I walk down the street every third car parked beside the pavement has a bomb in it and just as I am passing it explodes right from the centre out. Bang. The sides and front and back of the car are blown out and the roof just lifts right up and carries on rising. I'm not aware of it ever landing. I look over my right shoulder exactly at the moment it disintegrates. There is this loud bang, extremely loud but I manage to hear it without it destroying my eardrums and I look at the glare and dust and speed of the whole thing managing to have it all within my focus. My stomach and heart and lungs lurch a bit and then they settle back to normal. My feet do a little sideways jump and all the bits of car fly everywhere, faster than cricket balls but none of them touch me. Bits of upholstery and plastic carrier bags and jagged bits of tins of cat food, half a leather shoe, an ashtray with dog-ends in it and whole, great big bits of wing and door zoom through the air and there's a shower of glass like someone was throwing it around like confetti. I am as near to it as I am to you now. I'm nearer. It's barely a matter of feet. I mean pavements aren't that big are they? There's only about two, three feet between you and a parked car isn't there? And I'm right beside it, adjacent to it, to the tiny space between the front and back doors and the whole thing is blasted to Kingdom Come; the sort of thing that brought down whole houses in the war, sent people diving for shelter under their pianos and I get off scot-free. I'm not even scratched. I've got some dust and fluff and stuff up my nose and as I walk away I rub my eyes a bit 'cos they've got smuts in them but basically I'm completely OK. I'm just a bit grubby but that's not a problem is it? You change your clothes regularly as a matter of course, have a bath, blow your nose, don't you? . . . I'm not even frightened any more that there are bombs all over the place. I've just got accustomed to it. I think everyone has, no matter where they live. If there aren't actually bombs where you are, there sure as hell are bombs somewhere else aren't there? What's the difference? I mean somebody's getting blown up by a bomb they didn't expect this very minute and the truth is they knew there was a bomb there really. The fact it took them by surprise just means they'd forgotten about it temporarily, but they knew. We all know.

She picks up the phone and starts dialling. She stops and puts it down.

No, fuck it. Why should I?

HANNAH. What?

CHRIS. I was going to phone Stellios.

HANNAH. I didn't think that was still on.

CHRIS. I want to phone someone.

HANNAH. Phone your Mum.

CHRIS. I want to phone someone in America or something.

HANNAH. Phone Hugo. He'll talk to you.

CHRIS. Why? He's your boyfriend.

HANNAH. Go on.

CHRIS. Alright but I'm not going to talk to him.

CHRIS *dials a number.*

So are you back with Stellios?

CHRIS. What does that mean?

HANNAH. I thought you'd stopped seeing him.

CHRIS. He's my fuck.

HANNAH. Charming.

CHRIS. I only say it to annoy you.

HANNAH. It's tacky.

CHRIS. He's not there. (*She puts the phone down.*)

HANNAH. What time is it?

CHRIS. Midnight.

HANNAH. Is it?

CHRIS. Dunno. Why don't you look at your watch?

HANNAH. He'll be in bed.

CHRIS. Probably . . . I'm not living with him. I'm not going to marry him for God's sake. It's completely stationary. It's not going to go anywhere at all but . . . I can't get out of it at the moment.

HANNAH. You could.

CHRIS. Oh don't be holier than thou. Just because you've been with Hugo since university. It's not that easy.

HANNAH. You could and you should. You should get out of it if you don't want to be in it. It's not fair on Stellios.

CHRIS. He's my fuck. I'm his. Why should I feel guilty about that? Why should I give that up?

HANNAH. Because it makes you miserable.

Pause.

CHRIS. You know I don't *ever* remember having a boyfriend with money.

HANNAH. It's not doing you any good at all.

CHRIS. Dead right it isn't. I could handle a Colin now, something eligible with prospects.

HANNAH. I've never had a boyfriend with money either.

CHRIS. You've only ever been with Hugo.

HANNAH. 'Suppose so.

CHRIS. I don't know how you put up with him: he doesn't earn a thing.

HANNAH. He does.

CHRIS. What?

HANNAH. He earned eight thousand last year. Or something like that.

CHRIS. That's nothing.

HANNAH. It's all he needs: if he was teaching full time he wouldn't have enough time to do the things he wants so there wouldn't be any point, would there? He put our bed up on a platform last week. It's wonderful. At least it will be when . . .

CHRIS (*interrupts*). I mean money money. I mean wealth. I mean the credit card brigade.

HANNAH. Hugo's been potholing today.

CHRIS. I will get out of it. I just don't want to be on my own at the moment.

HANNAH. You want to be with someone who knows what they're doing.

CHRIS. Where do you meet them? You don't meet people being a waitress. You're invisible. . . . Christ! Who'd have thought I'd end up having a scene with the washer upper from the Greek?

HANNAH. You've got to get out of it.

CHRIS. He's sweet.

HANNAH. You've got to get out of being a waitress.

CHRIS. I know. I know. I know.

HANNAH. What you need to . . .

CHRIS. Don't give me advice.

HANNAH. You could . . .

CHRIS. I've missed the boat. I've never found anything I wanted to do. It's not easy. I . . .

HANNAH. There's no need . . .

CHRIS. Oh give it a rest. This is a weekend away. Right? So don't phone Hugo and see if he's managing without you and don't tell me what to do.

HANNAH. I'm not.

CHRIS. Yes you are.

HANNAH. I'm not.

CHRIS. You're on the verge.

Pause.

HANNAH. I think your handbag should match your shoes.

CHRIS. God no. That's absolutely fascinating. It's got thought in it.

HANNAH. British telephone directories are in four volumes.

CHRIS. The people in the flat above us are called Barbara and Simon.

HANNAH. My last car was an Escort.

CHRIS. *No.*

HANNAH. Why not?

CHRIS. Because you're left wondering what your present car is, how come you sold the old one. You can get infinitely more boring than that.

HANNAH. Your turn.

CHRIS. What are you doing?

HANNAH. Lying still.

CHRIS. What for?

HANNAH. Just for the hell of it.

CHRIS. Some friends of mine have just had a holiday in Cornwall.

HANNAH. I know a couple who are very fond of Eastbourne.

CHRIS. My brother's house has got gas-fired central heating.

HANNAH. My brother-in-law lives in Kingston.

CHRIS. That's pretty good.

HANNAH. We've got to crack it. We've got to come up with the most boring statement in the world. I want to have the most mega-boring statement at my fingertips so I've got it there poised, ready to drop into animated chat when I'm trapped talking to those people who talk house prices and mortgages and salaries and wall-to-wall carpeting and the benefits of the hatchback and . . .

CHRIS (*interrupts*). The B54 goes through Bromley.

HANNAH. Oh yes, that's a killer. That's in a league of its own. Brilliant. The B54 goes through Bromley. (*She sits up in her enthusiasm.*)

CHRIS. I don't know if it does.

HANNAH. Even better. You could have an incredibly boring conversation about whether it does or not and if it doesn't then where it does go through. (*She looks at her watch.*) I haven't moved for . . . 23 minutes. Imagine that for a lifetime. Christ! Not being able to move at all. Not being able to get up and wander around. (*She gets up and pours herself a whisky.*)

CHRIS. I don't want these intrusions in my life. I want to be a completely happy person without a care in the world. I don't want to be thinking of a girl's body lying in a shallow grave when I'm trying to remember how to make mince pies or I'm out spending money on myself. There are people who love spending money aren't there? They just love it. *Getting things.* It doesn't matter a monkey's what it is so long as they are out there getting something which is *new.*

She takes a large, red felt-tip pen out of her bag, which is on or about the sofa. She draws a large, open mouth on the television screen, teeth and all.

I'm such a sodding misery guts I don't even enjoy that. For a kick-off I get filled with guilt that I've got the money to part with while there's a child's body, an unidentified child's body decomposing in a wood not a million miles away from the stereo shop or the shoe shop. It really is fucking difficult to enjoy yourself and the News doesn't help. All the good news is above my head, all the stuff about money . . . I mean who knows what the Financial Times Share Index is?

HANNAH. The Financial Times Share Index . . .

CHRIS (*interrupts*). I just get weighed down with the man who got shot on the aeroplane and all the faces of people you know have died since the photos were taken. And the little girl whose father stuck his head in the oven and the lunatics out there who stick a gun in your face on a train. Jesus Christ I'd be a whole lot better off concentrating on working out what the Financial Times Share Index was and turning the ruddy thing off when it got to shallow graves, premature deaths and infants with inoperable heart disease.

HANNAH. The Financial Times Share Index tells some people how much money they've got. You haven't got any so that's why you don't know.

CHRIS. God I wish I had some money, I really do. What I couldn't do with a hundred pounds, two hundred pounds, fifty quid. I don't care.

HANNAH. You have got fifty quid.

CHRIS. I know.

HANNAH. If you invested fifty quid you'd make . . .

CHRIS (*interrupts*). I keep hearing that 'Lady'.

HANNAH. . . . five pounds a year.

CHRIS. 'Lady'.

HANNAH. Big deal.

CHRIS. 'Lady'.

HANNAH. What?

CHRIS. That dickhead on the train.

HANNAH. That happened weeks ago.

CHRIS. I know but I keep thinking about it . . . I just can't take it that things like that can happen every day.

HANNAH. They can but they don't.

CHRIS. But they always might. It made me so angry.

HANNAH. If that's the nearest you've been to disaster, you're lucky.

CHRIS. People get murdered on trains: things happen all the time.

HANNAH. Nothing did happen though did it?

CHRIS. A bloody lunatic stuck a gun in my face because I was looking 'serious'.

HANNAH. I don't believe it. Is that what he said?

CHRIS. How can you sort the real from the mental with that sort of thing going on?

HANNAH. I didn't think it was a gun I thought it was . . .

CHRIS (*interrupts*). Who cares what it was? I was bloody
_terrified.

HANNAH. You don't let these things go: that's your trouble.

CHRIS. God I know what I'd say if I saw him again.

HANNAH. Well you could travel on that bit of railway line for
the next ten years and never see him again so you might as
well forget it.

CHRIS. That's exactly it isn't it? You never know who you're
going to come across, what lunatics are out there lurking.

HANNAH. Nope . . . If I had been Bluebeard's wife and he'd
given me all those keys and told me I could go and play in all
the rooms except one special room which under no
circumstances was I to go into, I would have said, 'OK, that's
fine by me. Have it your own way.' And I'd have taken the keys
and with a hop, a skip and a jump I'd have been off round the
castle having a jolly good looksee. Then I'd have chosen the
room I liked the best: the room with the most light, the best
view and the least ghastly furniture. Then I'd have locked the
door, removed the key from the hundred or so other keys on
the key ring, hidden it where only I could possibly find it and
returned the rest to my childish spouse. He wouldn't have
ended up murdering me . . . What's Colin's wife like?

CHRIS. No idea.

HANNAH. Haven't you ever met her?

CHRIS. No. I don't know him well you know. I'm certainly not
in on the domestic bliss stuff.

HANNAH. What do you think she's like?

CHRIS. I think she's foreign.

HANNAH. I'm just trying to imagine the kind of person who'd
do that to a bathroom.

CHRIS *has now finished the mouth on the television screen and sits
back to admire it.*

CHRIS. There! A conceptual piece entitled, 'Mouth on a
television screen, inanimate' and 'Mouth on a television
screen, animate'. (*She switches the television on and then off.*)

HANNAH. Very clever. Have you signed it?

CHRIS (*doing it*). Yes.

HANNAH. Now you can clean it off. They're a bit of an enigma this Colin and his wife aren't they?

CHRIS. Rich people always are.

HANNAH. 'Suppose so. He must like you.

CHRIS. I have no idea.

HANNAH. How do you know him anyway?

CHRIS. I don't really. I knew him when I was seventeen. He was my boyfriend with a car. I wouldn't know him at all now 'cept he comes into the restaurant. He always expects special treatment 'cos we're old friends.

HANNAH. Well you are in a way.

CHRIS. Like hell we are. We've got nothing in common at all except background. He doesn't really want me staying here. He just blurted it out as a terribly funny thing to say to his turdy friends. 'Chris'd love to stay in an empty flat by the sea wouldn't you Chris?' So I said 'Yes'. So here we are. I don't know anything about him and he doesn't know anything about me. He just thinks he does. I know nothing about him but that doesn't stop me from knowing everything about him that you need to know 'cos you don't need to know anything about someone like that to know them inside out. He's rich. He probably goes sailing. He knows what the Financial Times Share Index is.

HANNAH. I'm sure he's got something he can find to worry about.

CHRIS. He's not concerned though. You never get people like him concerned about anything. He might dish out cheques to charity and feel he's a fucking saint but he's not going to be losing sleep over anything.

HANNAH. I don't know.

CHRIS. He's not. I'm telling you. I know him.

HANNAH. I thought you said you didn't.

CHRIS. They're all the same those people whatever they're like. They've got the passport to immunity. They're rich. They're making thousands and thousands of pounds, untold amounts of money and they're smiling all the time. Whenever you see them they're smiling. Great big grins looking straight at the camera. And you know when they move out of the picture

they'll be going somewhere nice. They're somewhere nice
already and they're going somewhere else that's nice and
next week they'll be going somewhere nice and the week after
that. They only ever go to nice places. And they have photos
taken a lot by their friends and by other people who want to
show us where these kind of people spend their weekends
and evenings and working lives and where they sleep because
all these places are nice so they are worth taking photos of.
They never have to live under a cloud like the rest of us. If the
area they're living in starts turning into a slum they can leave.
If they're gloomy about the stock exchange or the falling
pound or their lack of suntan they can go on holiday. What
about the rest of us? If you haven't got money you can't buy
yourself out of anything. How are you meant to cope?

HANNAH. I don't feel I'm under a cloud.

CHRIS. It's always there. We can always see it. We're never
under it. We're always safe, just about. It might be thousands
and thousands of miles away and we're watching it on the
telly. But we're watching it. It's out there, the disaster
looming over other disasters: the one that makes Noah's
Flood look like a damp patch in the bathroom. We all know
what's happening. That's what I can't bear. We all know.
Everything I know. I wish I didn't know what I know.

HANNAH. Then don't watch.

CHRIS. If we're not supposed to watch it why do they waste time
telling us everything in such immediate and vital and pressing
detail? If it's not supposed to mean anything why do they
make sure we learn about it *as soon as it's happened*? Pretty
much anything could be put right nowadays couldn't it?
We've got aeroplanes and plenty of food and drugs. There's
no need to be hell bent on disaster at all. It's not as if we were
still a bunch of medieval peasants roaming the world who
thought whatever it was was God's doing and therefore out of
our control. We know it isn't out of our control: we could put
things right and we don't. I should have lived in the middle
ages, before people even realised the world was round. I
could have coped with things then because whatever *was*
happening then *was* God's doing. Who was it making the
elements wreak havoc if not him? There weren't reasons for
things so no one was to blame. You could just feel terribly
sorry for everyone. You could make a whole way of life out of
trying hard against odds which you knew were safely beyond

your control. I'll bet it wasn't all that difficult, not inconceivable at least to feel a bit like a saint then, feeling that sorry for everyone and knowing with absolute certainty that all you could possibly do was try your best to help. That's what I should have been. I should have been a saint.

HANNAH. I tell you what Colin worries about. He worries about his money. At least you and I don't have to do that.

CHRIS. But it isn't the same now because God's on the telly. He's a bunch of self-appointed heroes on the Six o'clock News and News at Ten and plenty of other programmes. *Whenever* you turn on the telly it's the News. It's always the News . . . Why are you wearing my trousers?

HANNAH. I didn't think you'd mind.

CHRIS. I don't.

HANNAH. The difference is . . .

CHRIS. What difference?

HANNAH. The difference between you and other people is you're not getting blown up by a bomb at the moment and some poor sod is. Why imagine it until it happens?

CHRIS. You're a fine one to talk.

HANNAH. Meaning?

CHRIS. What were you doing imagining yourself paralysed? . . . That is what you were doing isn't it?

HANNAH. Yup.

CHRIS. So?

HANNAH. Dunno.

CHRIS. Well then.

HANNAH. I was counting myself lucky I'm not paralysed and touching wood I don't ever get to be.

CHRIS. You shouldn't put yourself through thinking things like that.

HANNAH. It's good for you. It's important to realise how lucky you are. Everything we've got works. We're terribly lucky.

CHRIS (*turning the television on*). What did I tell you? It's the News. (*Turning the television off.*) . . . When you're paralysed you can move a bit. You can always move something.

HANNAH. I know. I just thought I'd see what it felt like.

CHRIS. It's hard to make sense of things isn't it?

HANNAH. God, I don't waste my time trying to make sense of it.

CHRIS. You must do. How can you live with it unless you do?

HANNAH. Because I don't have to. I'm alright. It's not a problem.

CHRIS. You've got Multiple Sclerosis.

HANNAH. So what? You're a waitress and you hate it and you want a BMW and you're never going to get one and you're all knotted up inside.

CHRIS. Stand up. (HANNAH *does*.) They don't fit you.

HANNAH. They do.

CHRIS. They don't.

HANNAH. I don't care. They're comfy.

CHRIS. Wouldn't you like to be rich, just for five minutes? Wouldn't you like to have that option? . . . Know it was a possibility.

HANNAH. I have never thought I was poor.

CHRIS. There's no one else in the whole of Western Europe who could live like you and say that.

HANNAH. It's true. What matters to me is my own personal happiness. What do I need more money for? It wouldn't help me with learning Spanish would it? I know when I get back from Nicaragua next year everyone'll be telling me how amazing I am and how much they'd love to travel themselves. But they don't and they've got far more money than me. I've never found there was anything I couldn't do that I wanted to do because I didn't have the money. But then I've never wanted a fitted kitchen or a BMW and I'd be bored to death in a five-star hotel.

CHRIS. But in a five-star hotel there'd be a video: you wouldn't have to watch the News.

HANNAH. I've been to South America. I've walked through Nepal. What the hell do I want to sit in a hotel bedroom for?

You know the big question?

CHRIS. What?

HANNAH. Is it wiser in this world to be cautious or to throw caution to the wind?

CHRIS. I dunno.

HANNAH. Exactly. You could be buggered either way so it doesn't matter which you choose. Do what makes you happy.

CHRIS. I'm going to do something tomorrow, I've decided.

HANNAH. What?

CHRIS. I dunno yet.

HANNAH. Great.

CHRIS. I'm going to be in a good mood tomorrow.

HANNAH. I can't wait. (*Looking at the drawing on the television.*) Is that going to come off?

CHRIS. Dunno.

HANNAH. Daft prat.

CHRIS. I thought you'd approve. You hate telly.

HANNAH. I know but it's not yours.

CHRIS. Oh dear. I forgot.

Blackout.

Scene Three

Friday night 4 a.m.

Moonlight. CHRIS *enters. She is in nightclothes.* LUGGAGE *enters through a wall and with her comes some light. She is of course carrying her suitcase.*

CHRIS. Four o'clock in the bloody morning. Again.

LUGGAGE. Yes.

CHRIS. Bewildered.

LUGGAGE. Yes.

CHRIS. Bad tempered.

LUGGAGE. Yes.

CHRIS. Very bad tempered . . . Angry. Resentful. Confused. Frustrated.

LUGGAGE. Yes.

CHRIS. Paranoid.

LUGGAGE. Yes.

CHRIS. And . . . no that's it.

LUGGAGE. You can still enjoy your journey.

CHRIS. All I've got to do is change. ⎫ (*The words are*

LUGGAGE. . . . . accept. ⎬ *said simultaneously.*)

CHRIS. What?

LUGGAGE. Accept.

CHRIS. I always feel barmy in the middle of the night. (*She switches the television on.*) You can watch this 24 hours a day now; sound up, sound down.

LUGGAGE. Listen. (*She switches off the television.*) My mother told me to carry this suitcase over the mountain. So I did. And when I got to the other side she was there waiting for me and she told me to turn round and carry the suitcase straight back to where I had just come from. I was exhausted and very hungry but it was her will: so I did. I shifted my suitcase from my left hand to my right for my left arm was wearying under the heavy burden. I tightened my grip, took a deep breath and set off. And when I got back she was already there, standing with her arm outstretched and her finger pointing back over the mountain.

So I turned again and with every inch of my body weeping with fatigue I started to climb. Every other step I took I had to change arms. Every boulder I reached I had to spur myself on to make the effort to get to the next. But I couldn't carry on. And there was no one to talk to. So I talked to God. And he answered me. And I knew I had to go on, that I had been put on the earth to climb that mountain and bear my burden with fortitude. Only in accepting my suffering would I realise my whole purpose in life. And I looked up, strong and enriched with God's love. I carried past the next two, three, ten boulders and over the top and down the other side with my heart pounding with joy.

And when I got there she was there. And she was stamping and shouting and very excited. And she grabbed the suitcase from me and pulled it open so the contents spilled out on to the ground. They formed a neat little mound – of rubble. White, chalky stones. And she stood back and laughed and laughed and through her tears and somewhat short of breath she said, 'There, hasn't that made Madam angry?' And I said 'No.' Because it hadn't: but it had made her angry somehow. She stopped laughing instantly and pointed out across the mountain. So I turned and began again.

And I found the more I climbed my mountain, for I carried on climbing my mountain for many years, the more I had God by my side to give me the strength. I had found my purpose. If my father had not abused me, and my mother punished me for it, I would never have found the Lord. My purpose was to accept that suffering. And I did. With joy.

And yet my burden never lessened because the more I did my mother's will the more angry she became. I could never please her. My faith made her angry and yet it was only my faith which gave me the strength to do her will. Poor mother could have been so much happier if she had sought God's help. She was never relieved of her anger.

CHRIS. Your father abused you?

LUGGAGE. Yes.

CHRIS. And your mother punished you for it?

LUGGAGE. Yes.

CHRIS. And you accepted that?

LUGGAGE. God gave me the strength: I could only endure my burden if I accepted it.

CHRIS. If I believed in God, would I find the world less sad?

LUGGAGE. With God's help you would be able to cope with your sadness.

CHRIS. I don't want to cope with it. I want it to go away.

LUGGAGE. My mother wanted her anger to go away . . .

CHRIS (*interrupts*). That too.

LUGGAGE. She never understood that her anger was her burden because she never found God's love to give her the strength to see that truth and accept it.

CHRIS (*yawning*). I wish I knew where my mountain was and all I had was a suitcase.

LUGGAGE. You will be able to see it if you let go of that anger, if you let go of that frustration, if you let got of that paranoia, if . . .

CHRIS (*interrupts, still yawning*). It's not as simple as that any more. We all know everything now. You can never go on holiday from it. (*Exiting.*) When I get to Heaven I'm going to be a saint too. I'm going to be patron saint of insomnia. And anger. And dread. And . . . (*Exits.*).

LUGGAGE *crosses her suitcase from her right hand to her left and sets off through a wall.*

Blackout

Scene Four

Saturday 10 a.m.

It is bright morning light. CHRIS *is talking to Stellios on the telephone.*

CHRIS. It's alright. It got us here. But it's no BMW . . . . We had a takeaway and got a bit pissed . . . there's nothing to cook on . . . Because Hannah won't . . . Oh I don't know: she hates spending money. You'd stay in a hotel wouldn't you? . . . I did ask you. Oh let's not get into this one Stellios . . . Anyway you wouldn't want to be here, honestly, it's like a barn . . . a barn . . . It means it's cold. It's like where they put horses . . . Animals. Pigs. You know. I'd much rather be in your room in . . . Ummn? I don't know. It must be twelve or something . . . Oh is it? Sorry, I didn't realise . . . You can sleep in a minute . . . Big deal: I haven't slept all night . . . You can sleep the rest of the morning. You can sleep the whole bloody day . . . I'm really tired too. This is my weekend away . . . I might. But I might be out . . . Yeah. It's great. I'm enjoying myself. It's fine . . . Ten o'clock is *not* too early to phone people.

She slams the phone down. PEST *enters through a wall. He is holding his air pistol. It is pointed at her. He is dressed as before.*

PEST. Lady . . . Lady . . . Lady.

CHRIS. Ummn?

PEST. Lady.

CHRIS. Yes.

PEST. Here. Look. Lady.

CHRIS. What?

PEST. Look.

CHRIS. What?

PEST. What's this?

CHRIS (*she looks up*). A . . .

PEST. That's right.

CHRIS. It's a . . .

PEST. Right . . . What is it?

CHRIS. It's a gun.

PEST. A what?

CHRIS. A gun.

PEST. What is it?

CHRIS. A gun.

PEST. What?

CHRIS. Gun.

PEST. What?

CHRIS. It's a gun.

PEST. Nah, it isn't.

CHRIS. What do you want?

PEST. Nothing.

CHRIS. Oh, yes?

PEST. Yeah.

CHRIS. I know what you want.

PEST. What's that?

CHRIS. Get out of my head and go and plague somebody else.
    I'm not in the mood.

PEST. Look.

CHRIS. I'm not.

PEST. *Bang.*

CHRIS. Are you deaf or just stupid?

PEST. Stupid.

CHRIS. I'm not in the mood. I only just got here. I'm on my weekend away. I'm here to enjoy myself.

PEST. Yeah?

CHRIS. Yes.

PEST. Doing what?

CHRIS. I don't know. Something.

PEST. What?

CHRIS. I'm not here to watch the News and let my mind run amok. I don't have to think about you or guns or anything. My brain doesn't have to be on the edge. I can make my mind a blank. Other people do. I can.

PEST. Do you reckon there's blanks in this?

CHRIS. What?

PEST. Were you scared?

CHRIS. There's nothing going on in my head at all. Go and pester somebody else.

PEST. Who?

CHRIS. I don't know.

He switches on the television. CHRIS *switches it off.*

PEST. Oh go on.

CHRIS. Sod off or I'll throw it out of the window.

PEST. Not very friendly are you?

CHRIS. Sod off or I'll throw myself out with it. Then you'll be at a loose end won't you?

PEST *turns the television back on.* CHRIS *turns it off.*

Go and play in the traffic. That should be right up your street.

PEST. There isn't any.

CHRIS. Well go and detonate a mine. There must be one out

there on the beach somewhere. Just get out of my head.

PEST. Why were you frightened?

CHRIS. You stuck a gun in my face.

PEST. It's not a gun. It's a . . .

CHRIS (*interrupts*). Go and plague somebody else.

PEST. I wanna plague you.

CHRIS. Why?

PEST. 'Cos you like it.

CHRIS. I loathe it.

PEST. Why do you always come back for more then? You're paranoid twenty-four hours a day. You're ready for a hit all the time.

CHRIS. I'm on holiday. I'm going to enjoy myself in spite of the state of my head.

PEST. I'll just hang about. I'll be quiet. I won't do anything. I'll just lurk.

CHRIS. What for?

PEST. I'll just wait.

CHRIS. What for?

PEST. You know.

CHRIS. What?

PEST. 'Til you're ready.

CHRIS. What for?

PEST. Bit of fun.

CHRIS. Right. That's it.

PEST. Something's going to get you wound up soon. You're going to be sitting there watching telly and the News is going to come on and something's going to really piss you off and I'll be right there and . . .

CHRIS (*interrupts*). I'm going to recite every town I can think of in Britain that starts with B . . .

PEST. But it's not going to hit you really 'cos it's a game. This is a game. (*Holds up the gun.*). Look. You know it's a game. So what are you frightened for?

CHRIS. Bolton. Basingstoke. Bath. Berwick-on-Tweed. Biggin Hill.

PEST. That's not a town.

CHRIS. Brighton. Beer. Bournemouth. Bristol. Birmingham.

PEST. Shit.

He exits through a wall. The phone goes. CHRIS *crosses to the television and turns it on. She sits down to watch. On about the eighth ring we hear someone rush up the stairs. The door bursts open and* HANNAH *falls through it. The phone stops ringing.* HANNAH *is carrying a tent.*

HANNAH. Why didn't you answer?

CHRIS. I thought it was you.

HANNAH. Liar.

CHRIS. I did.

HANNAH. Why would I phone you?

Pause.

Ummn?

CHRIS. I dunno. I thought you might be phoning from the beach for a laugh.

HANNAH. Why would I phone you? I can talk to you any time.

CHRIS. Dunno.

HANNAH. Come on. Why would I phone you?

CHRIS. For a chat. I dunno.

HANNAH *switches off the television.*

HANNAH. You don't even want to get up, let alone have a chat.

CHRIS. We chat.

HANNAH. Why didn't you answer?

CHRIS. I don't want to talk to anyone. Who was it anyway?

HANNAH. How would I know?

CHRIS. What do you want to answer it for then?

HANNAH. It was ringing.

CHRIS. So?

HANNAH. So you answer it.

CHRIS. You don't have to . . . Do you?

HANNAH. Obviously not.

Pause. HANNAH *starts to unfold and attempt to put up the tent. She is basically occupied, although often distracted, with doing this until the job is completed.*

What have you been doing?

CHRIS. Nothing.

HANNAH. You haven't decided what you're going to do with your life?

CHRIS. Very funny.

HANNAH. I don't know what's happening to you Chris but you're certainly not helping yourself. You're . . .

CHRIS (*interrupts*). You're going to tell me what to do.

HANNAH. Yes I am.

CHRIS. We made a pact.

HANNAH. I don't care.

CHRIS. No telling me what to do with my life over this weekend.

HANNAH. I think you should go back to being a courier.

CHRIS. What?

HANNAH. It's the only thing you've ever liked doing. You've told me dozens of times. You liked it much more than teaching English as a foreign language. You stuck being a courier for two years or something didn't you? And you did it when you got back from Australia. Why don't you just do that?

CHRIS. Showing nitwits round Europe is what you do when you leave university. It's a holiday job. You wouldn't settle for that for five minutes.

HANNAH. I'm not talking about me.

CHRIS. Would you?

HANNAH. No.

CHRIS. So what are you telling me to do it for? Why you want to answer a call that couldn't possibly be for you beats me.

HANNAH. You're really pissing me off you know.

CHRIS. Nobody knows we're here.

HANNAH. So? . . . Colin knows we're here doesn't he?

CHRIS *picks up the receiver and puts it down on the floor.*

CHRIS. It goes dead after a while.

HANNAH *puts the receiver back on the phone.*

HANNAH. You can't do that.

CHRIS. Why not?

HANNAH. Because there are people trying to get us.

CHRIS. Exactly.

HANNAH. Because after a while the line goes dead and then no one can get in touch with you and then everyone reports the phone out of order and people come round to repair it and find that actually there's nothing wrong with it and then it all gets in a muddle because the phone people send you bills for mending a phone which wasn't even broken in the first place because technically speaking they did mend it because they made the journey to mend it even if it wasn't broken and there wasn't anything for them to do when they got here. And it isn't even your phone to piss around with. It's Colin's and he's not here. I'm buggered if I'm going to enter into endless bloody boring negotiations with the phone people because you get your knickers in a twist every time the thing rings.

CHRIS. Don't get hysterical.

HANNAH. Well sod it, it's so trivial.

CHRIS. It's not bloody trivial. It drives me round the bend.

HANNAH. How can you sit there at eleven o'clock in the morning watching television I don't know.

CHRIS. I don't feel normal. I go outside and burst into tears. It's too beautiful or too big. . . . I'm going to have a bath.

HANNAH. Another?

CHRIS. Ummn?

HANNAH. You were in the bath when I went out.

CHRIS. Was I?

HANNAH. All you've done today is have a bath and watch telly.

CHRIS. The last thing I want to do is watch television and I can't seem to make myself do anything else. All day, every day there are people dying and going through hell. How are we supposed to cope?

HANNAH *crosses over to the window.*

HANNAH. Look at that! God, look at that! There's a man standing on the beach. He's just standing there. He must be mad. Doesn't he know what he's doing? He's going to be struck by lightning if he's not careful. A bull's going to get out of a field 50 miles away and make straight for him. You'd better get out there. You might miss it.

CHRIS *goes over to the window.*

CHRIS. I'm going off my trolley you know. I don't remember having a bath at all.

HANNAH. See? There's absolutely nothing happening out there. No clouds in the sky and no people on the beach: the British idea of the perfect holiday spot. Whatever's happening's happening on the telly. You don't know the bloke who got shot on the aeroplane do you? What's he to you? You can't feel for everyone.

CHRIS. I'm not feeling for everyone. I'm not just frightened of all the global catastrophe out of the goodness of my heart, on everyone else's behalf. I'm frightened for me as well. Lightning does strike you know.

HANNAH. You wanted peace and quiet. You've got it. You don't seem to be able to see it. There aren't even any loonies out there. It's safe. Listen . . . You can hear it's safe. It smells safe. There's absolutely nothing happening out there apart from a couple of dogs sniffing each other's bums.

CHRIS. I feel completely numb: right the way through my body and my head as well. It's like I'm made of suet or something. I can't make anything work properly. Sorry, I shouldn't say things like that.

HANNAH. Why?

CHRIS. No, I'm sorry.

HANNAH. Doesn't bother me. It seems to be impossible for you to fathom but I don't feel that bothered about it because I don't actually know what it is that I've got to feel that bothered about.

CHRIS. I think you're very brave about it. I couldn't . . .

HANNAH (*interrupts*). Stop talking shit and sounding all portentous. You couldn't what? How do you know? I'll tell you about it seeing you've brought it up. There are no two people the same who've got Multiple Sclerosis. But basically there are some people who are alright and others who aren't and I'm one of the lucky ones. I was ill for six months but I'm perfectly alright now. I could very well be OK for the rest of my life. But I'm frail. I'm on God's hit list and I need to take care. And the way you take care is by trying to be bloody happy. It really pisses me off seeing you sit there, the Prophet of Doom . . .

CHRIS. Sorry.

HANNAH. Anyone can make you cry for them, illness or no illness. Everyone's on their own or desperate or insecure or pathetic or something but they're not showing it. That's what keeps us all going. I could get terribly depressed. We all could. Some people make a whole way of life out of it. 'How are you doing?' 'I'm really depressed.' 'Are you?' 'Yup. Really depressed. How are you?' 'I don't know. I'm pretty depressed I suppose.' 'Are you?' 'Yup.' 'It's really depressing isn't it?' 'Yup.' 'I get so depressed. Why are you so depressed?' 'Dunno. It's just all so depressing.' *Christ*! It's enough to drive anyone demented.

CHRIS. Sorry.

HANNAH (*displaying the tent*). What do you think? Ten quid.

CHRIS. A snip. A bargain.

HANNAH. The lady said there might be a couple of pegs missing but what the hell, ten quid. It's incredible what people throw away. You can get almost anything if you're prepared to wait. You've just got to keep your eyes open and there it'll be sitting in a skip at the side of the road or turning up in a jumble sale or . . .

CHRIS. Do you want a tent?

HANNAH. I dunno. But you can't look a gift-horse in the mouth can you? You should have been there. This is the kind

of place to go to a jumble sale. It was a designer jumble sale of
the first order. Who'd chuck out something like this?

CHRIS. Rich people.

HANNAH. Ummn?

CHRIS. Rich people don't need tents and sleeping bags and
stuff do they? They don't have those sorts of holiday.

HANNAH. Suppose so.

CHRIS. That's how you play at being rich.

HANNAH. How?

CHRIS. You chuck things out . . . And you give whopping
cheques to charity.

HANNAH. No. You buy a bottle of champagne . . . no . . . you
have a bottle of champagne and you use it to wash your hair
. . . no . . . you use it to wash your husband's hair . . . and he's
bald.

The front door opens. TUNIS *stands in the doorway, her arms
weighed down by two pairs of curtains. The instant impression she
creates is of a woman who derives a great deal of her confidence in life
and with men from the way she looks, from the way she makes herself
look. She is very young, early twenties, and not British. She is called*
TUNIS *because that is where she was conceived.*

TUNIS. So you *are* here. Have you an aversion to answering the
phone or something?

HANNAH. Hello.

TUNIS. Ummn?

CHRIS. Sorry?

TUNIS. Don't you believe in answering the phone?

CHRIS. Ummn . . .

TUNIS *comes into the room, unloads the curtains and sits down.*

TUNIS. No. No. Really. I can manage. They only weigh about a
ton and a half.

HANNAH. Sorry, I wasn't thinking.

TUNIS. I hope you're not thinking of leaving that there,
whatever it is.

HANNAH. It's a tent.

TUNIS. What's it doing there?

HANNAH. I was just trying it out . . . We're not in your way are we?

TUNIS. No. No. Don't worry. I'm Tunis.

CHRIS. Colin's wife?

TUNIS. No I just fell in off the street. Who else could I be?

HANNAH. I'm Hannah.

CHRIS. Chris.

TUNIS. Really? I thought you were Chris. Isn't that interesting.

HANNAH. Did you?

TUNIS. What on earth do you want to come and stay here for?

HANNAH. What do you mean?

TUNIS. Why would anyone want to come and stay here?

CHRIS. Colin invited us.

TUNIS. I know. But what is there to do all day?

HANNAH. Mooch about. It's nice.

CHRIS. There's masses to do.

TUNIS. You're both English aren't you?

HANNAH. Yes.

TUNIS. You'd have to be.

HANNAH. Would you like a cup of tea?

TUNIS. Why? I haven't had an accident. No thank you. I never drink tea. I thought you must have gone and stayed in a hotel.

CHRIS. It never crossed my mind.

TUNIS. Why not? I am. It's perfectly straightforward. You go in, leave your bags and get given a key to a room. It's one of life's easier tests. You can't have a holiday in an empty flat.

CHRIS. Colin obviously thought we could or he wouldn't have suggested it.

TUNIS. Do you think I could have a drink? Getting down here's been a nightmare.

HANNAH. I'm not sure there is any.

TUNIS. Don't you drink?

HANNAH. Yes of course. Umm . . .

TUNIS. People die in rooms like these, behind their net curtains. Did you know net curtains were invented by the English? Oh yes they were. There can be no doubt about that at all. Who will I ever find to talk to here? At least in Greece it's hot so you don't need to talk.

CHRIS. Would you like a whisky? That's all we've got.

TUNIS. Yes, that'd be wonderful.

CHRIS. Hannah?

HANNAH. Yes. Thanks.

CHRIS *exits through the interior door.*

HANNAH. This looks nice. (*Indicating the curtains.*)

TUNIS. They're curtains. Would you mind holding them up? Yes, let's have a look. Over there. By the window. You can go up the ladder. I'll be able to see them full. Yes that's right. I'll watch from over here. (HANNAH *holds up one of the curtains.*) So I can see it. (HANNAH *puts more effort into it.*) Open it right out.

HANNAH. I have.

CHRIS *enters with the whisky and glasses.*

TUNIS. Right out. Bigger.

HANNAH. I have. That's it.

TUNIS. It can't be.

HANNAH. It is.

Pause.

TUNIS. Fuck it. Fuck them. For fuck's sake. You can't trust anyone to do anything. Jesus, they're miles too small. Miles and miles and miles. I can't bear it. I'm going to have to do the whole thing again. I can't stand it. They're the very best people and they've fucked it up. At least if you employ someone really useless you know they're going to be really useless and they're going to do a really useless job so it won't come as a surprise. You don't expect that from people who know what they're doing. Bugger it. It's just a pair of bloody curtains. Why doesn't anything ever turn out right? They're absolutely bloody useless. I'm going to kill Miranda.

HANNAH. Are you sure?

TUNIS. Of course I'm sure. Can't you see?

HANNAH. No.

TUNIS. She said they were the *only* people, the *only* people in London. And look at the result. What a bloody waste of time. God I hate this place.

HANNAH. Maybe they'd look alright in the bedroom.

TUNIS. They weren't made for the bedroom.

HANNAH *relaxes her arms completely. Up to this point she has been half-heartedly holding the curtains up.* CHRIS *hands out the drinks.*

CHRIS. Cheers.

HANNAH. What will you do with them? They're beautiful curtains.

TUNIS. They'll have to make them again.

HANNAH *makes an attempt at folding the curtain.* TUNIS *goes and looks out of the window.*

Oh look. There's an old man out there jogging. Isn't that exciting.

Pause.

HANNAH. We drove down. Yesterday.

TUNIS. Do you know what is out there?

CHRIS. What?

TUNIS. France. And what is beyond France? Italy. And beyond Italy? Greece. And where have we chosen to buy a holiday flat? . . . The English Riviera.

CHRIS. I'm going out. (*To* HANNAH.) Do you want anything?

HANNAH. Ummn.

CHRIS. Think about it. (*Exits through the interior door.*)

HANNAH. You don't seem to like this flat at all.

TUNIS. It was Colin's bright idea. He has an obsession about the place. He's only been here once and that was to buy it. It's me who has to do all the work. But he says it's essential to him. He thinks we're going to get down here for quiet weekends. We haven't managed to get away once in the last six months. He's a workaholic. Are you married?

HANNAH. No.

TUNIS. Don't you want to marry?

HANNAH. Not necessarily.

TUNIS. Whatever you do it'll be wrong. When you marry you marry what you don't like as well as what you do and yet you probably never let yourself think about just how much you didn't like whatever it is you don't before you actually did it. Colin is never there. Honestly. It hasn't always been like this. I blame Japan. He got an enormous contract there last August. It feels like the last time I saw him alive.

HANNAH. Is he working today?

TUNIS. *And* last night. *And* tomorrow.

HANNAH. That's not good for him.

TUNIS. Phone him up and tell him. Please. It's driving me mad. He needs a break so badly. It's ridiculous. We were going to a lovely place just outside Oxford this weekend. I had my bag packed ready at the front door and he phoned me from the office to tell me it was off. We couldn't even have a row about it because he was in some meeting. So I just thought, 'Bugger it: I'll go and do the bloody flat'. If we didn't have this place we'd be free to have weekends in France . . . anywhere. We had some wonderful times when we first met. Longchamps on the spur of the moment. What am I talking about? He won't go anywhere, let alone somewhere nice.

HANNAH. I really like this place.

TUNIS. Do you?

HANNAH. Yes. My boyfriend would love it.

TUNIS. It does have potential. But getting it right is such hard work. You have to be *at* people all the time.

CHRIS *enters.*

CHRIS. I'm going shopping. (*Exits.*)

TUNIS. Don't you want to go?

HANNAH. Um. No not really. There's more to life than what's in the shops isn't there?

TUNIS. Not a lot.

HANNAH. Anyway I've been shopping already.

TUNIS. What did you get?

HANNAH. That tent.

TUNIS. Oh.

HANNAH. Ten quid. I can't believe it.

TUNIS. Is that good?

HANNAH. Brilliant.

TUNIS. I've never bought a tent.

HANNAH. What does Colin do?

TUNIS. He has his own company. I think that's really what the problem is. There's no limit to how hard he can work. He says it's going to ease up in the next few months. It's so frustrating I don't seem to be able to get through to him at all. Sorry I shouldn't be telling you all this.

HANNAH. That's alright.

TUNIS. We should be enjoying ourselves. It's only a matter of time before I have children. Life's too short. What's the point of having money if you don't take the time to enjoy it? Whenever I say that to Colin he has a fit saying if he took *that* kind of time we wouldn't have *this* kind of money. Whenever he's really under pressure he takes it out on me. He wants to know what I have been doing with my time; how I manage to fill my days doing nothing. Nobody does nothing.

HANNAH. No, that's true.

TUNIS. I'm *mad* about those curtains. England's alright apart from the weather. And the people. And the way of life. (*She takes out her makeup and mirror and retouches her makeup.*)

HANNAH. Doesn't leave a lot does it?

TUNIS. I'll never know what possessed me to fall in love with an Englishman. You'd have thought that after seven years of being frozen to death in an English boarding school I'd have had the sense to marry someone who lived somewhere hot. (*She has finished her makeup.*) Are you going to be here this afternoon?

HANNAH. I should think so.

TUNIS. Good, there are a couple of things being delivered.

HANNAH. I don't know I might . . .

TUNIS. OK. Don't worry about it. If there's no one here they'll just have to come back. And now I'm going to buy a mirror. That's what this room needs, a big mirror. At least then you'd be able to see yourself. I'm going to drive round listening to very loud music. I'm going to look in the antique shops and I'm going to spend money. It's what I'm expected to do. It's what I like doing and why shouldn't you do what you like? That's what's essential to me: my car. I'd die without my car.

Blackout.

Scene Five

Saturday 4 p.m.

Sound of ELLIOTT *trying to open the door. He succeeds and comes int the room holding a credit card which he puts in a pocket. He forgets to close the door. He crosses straight over to the sofa. He feels all around behind the cushions etc., looking for his jacket. He looks under the sofa and finds several empties. He pulls them out. He goes and rummages through the cupboard.* LUGGAGE *enters through a wall.*

ELLIOTT. My name is Elliott. John Spencer Elliott. I live at the Hathawden House Hotel, Brighton. I am in Brighton. (*Takes a newspaper out of his coat pocket and reads:*) Today is Saturday the 16th of October. I am divorced. My children's names are Patricia and Roger. My wife's name was Barbara. She went off with Brian. I was at Trinity. I was at Lloyds. I was in Hong Kong. The house is in Altrincham. My number plate is OUU 343T . . . I have been driving. . . My passport number is N77487. I had a bath on Tuesday. I met Malcolm. I came here on Wednesday. I've lost three days Luggage. I don't know where I've been. I don't know who I've been with. I don't know what I've been doing. (*He's getting a bit shaky.*)

LUGGAGE. Clothilde.

ELLIOTT. What happened to make me do it again? (*The shaking continues.*)

LUGGAGE. I don't know.

ELLIOTT. Nothing happened. It never does. It just happens.

He takes a large stone, originally from the beach, out of the cupboard. He wraps the bottles in the newspaper and starts to smash them with the stone.

I know I was here on Wednesday. I must have been to leave these. I shouldn't have left a mess. If you leave a thing as you find it it won't just catch up with you. My sodding jacket must be here. There's half my life in that jacket. I can't remember anything. Give me a clue.

LUGGAGE. I can't.

ELLIOTT. What can you do?

LUGGAGE. I can pray for you.

ELLIOTT. *And* who I am. Bloody Hell. If it isn't here it's . . . I came here on Wednesday. Can't you help?

LUGGAGE. I cannot carry your burden for you.

ELLIOTT. . . . just to piece it together.

LUGGAGE. I don't know anything.

ELLIOTT. My address book. Barbara's letter. My pictures of the children.

LUGGAGE. I can only be an example to you.

ELLIOTT. I still call them children.

LUGGAGE. We are all children.

ELLIOTT. I tried to be an example to them. I have always done my best. What more could I do? You can't do more than that.

LUGGAGE. Nobody can.

ELLIOTT. But they never understood that. I needed help too. It hasn't always been me making the wrong decisions. I'm not going to blame myself. I was up to here with pressure. I'm the one who's suffering . . . I need that bloody letter.

LUGGAGE. Accepting your suffering is a virtue.

ELLIOTT. Try telling that to my wife. Do I look like a complete bastard to you?

LUGGAGE. God gave us free will. We choose how we are. We make ourselves.

ELLIOTT. I didn't choose this.

LUGGAGE. We can all make mistakes with our free will.

ELLIOTT. I didn't.

LUGGAGE. Let me be an example to you. I was made the
Patron Saint of Heavy Burdens because I bore my own with
fortitude. I embraced my journey and because I did it gave
me joy.

ELLIOTT. It shouldn't be me who's got the bloody burden. I've
put in the work, the time, the money, the commitment and
I've always been let down. What I'll never understand is why
he didn't talk to me first. I've been in business all my life.
£30,000 would have been nothing to an import company like
ours. I could have got hold of that kind of figure in two days.
All we had to do was sit and wait. People are falling over
themselves for Australian wine now. We were a bit ahead of
the game that's all. But he panics, picks a name out of the
Sunday papers, phones them up and gives the whole shooting
match away to a bunch of cowboys. 'Don't worry, it's all
perfectly legal. Sign here. You can buy it all back later at a
price you can afford. We'll make an arrangement for you on
the Isle of Man.' What kind of an idiot do you have to be to
fall for that? It's left me so broke, I can't even afford to bloody
sue him. But he's feeling sorry for himself now he knows what
he's lost: he didn't deserve to have me for a partner. There's
never been anyone in the whole of my life who has
appreciated me. Oh, if only.

He sees and goes to pick up HANNAH'*s bottle of whisky.*

You're looking like my wife: long suffering. I could have done
with a little appreciation and support from her too but all I
got was, 'Look at the way you've parked that car!' I may drink
a touch more than I should but given the circumstances of
my life isn't it understandable? I've had more than my fair
share . . .

He picks up the bottle and realises it is half full.

God's in his heaven: all's well with the world.

He drinks.

Whose is this?

LUGGAGE. I don't know.

ELLIOTT. I never buy this.

LUGGAGE *exits through a wall.*

HANNAH (*off*). Now you're not to laugh. You've got to promise
me you're not going to laugh. This is makeup to go with Any
Outfit. Alright? Are you ready? (ELLIOTT *holds the bottle in his
left hand: it should be obscured by his coat.*) Promise? . . . Right.
(*She enters.*) Da Da! (*She has got herself made up in a department
store: that is what she has to show off.*) Jesus!

ELLIOTT. Hello.

HANNAH. How did you get in? Who are you?

ELLIOTT. Catherine isn't it? (*Extends his hand.*)

HANNAH. What?

ELLIOTT. How are you? You really want to be more careful with
the front door you know; especially round here. There are a
lot of doubtful characters about at this time of . . .

HANNAH (*interrupts*). How did you get in?

ELLIOTT. Didn't you mean to leave it open?

HANNAH. Jesus you gave me a fright. Who are you?

ELLIOTT. I've done that. It's a ghastly feeling isn't it when
you're half way to work and you know you've forgotten to lock
up properly? Never mind, there's nothing missing is there?

HANNAH. What are you doing here?

ELLIOTT. It is Catherine isn't it?

HANNAH. No it isn't.

ELLIOTT. Sorry, I've got a memory like a sieve. Didn't I meet
you here with Michael? A few weeks ago? At your . . . what
would you call it . . . pre-housewarming?

HANNAH. It's not my flat.

ELLIOTT. But you were here. I never forget a face. Names yes
but never faces. I came along with a colleague of mine who
wanted me to meet . . . what is the name of the chap who
owns this flat?

HANNAH. Colin.

ELLIOTT. Colin. That's right. Colin . . . because we're in the
same line of business.

HANNAH. What do you want?

ELLIOTT. I was just passing. I'm actually due at a meeting with some overseas clients shortly . . . (*Looks at his watch.*)

HANNAH. It's Saturday afternoon.

ELLIOTT. No rest for the wicked. I dropped in to see if they'd moved in and if by any chance they'd come across a jacket of mine. I've mislaid this jacket . . . the other half of this suit as it happens but there isn't that much of a chill in the air yet so I thought I could risk a day without a jacket but I would actually like to have it back. It's pretty idiotic having a pair of trousers with no flaming jacket to go with them isn't it?

HANNAH. A jacket?

ELLIOTT. Yes.

HANNAH. . . . You've left here?

ELLIOTT. Yes.

HANNAH. When?

ELLIOTT. Oh it must be . . . it must be . . .

HANNAH. I think it's in the kitchen.

ELLIOTT. Marvellous. Good girl.

HANNAH. Wait here.

She exits. ELLIOTT takes a quick drink. He puts the bottle down making sure it is within easy reach. HANNAH enters.

Is this it?

ELLIOTT. Yes indeed. The very one. Thank you. (*He takes it from her and checks it thoroughly. He takes a wallet out of an inside pocket and looks inside it. Satisfied, he replaces it and puts the jacket on.*) It must have been quite a party mustn't it?

HANNAH. What?

ELLIOTT. I must have had one too many . . .

HANNAH. Why?

ELLIOTT. . . . To go and leave my jacket behind.

HANNAH. Oh . . . yes. It's in a state. It's been in the . . .

ELLIOTT (*interrupts*). Not to worry. Nothing a good clean won't sort out.

HANNAH. Chris threw it out.

ELLIOTT. Chris of course. How is he?

HANNAH. Not bad.

ELLIOTT. I knew it was here. Silly I haven't been to retrieve it
before but you just get too bloody busy don't you? I'm not
really looking up to scratch for this meeting am I? You
wouldn't believe the household I've been staying in the last
couple of days: children, dogs . . . and the cat was sick over me
just as I was leaving this morning. They're lovely people but
the mess! I could hardly make my way to the front door.

HANNAH. Look I don't . . .

ELLIOTT (*interrupts*). I can't really afford the time to get back
to my hotel before this meeting so I'm just going to have to
. . . I should have put myself up in a decent hotel but they're
in difficulties financially at the moment and I wanted to see if
I could help them out in any way, you know. Every single
thing you can think of needs to be done to the house. I went
into the bathroom this morning for a shave and the bloody
tap splashed, literally sloshed water all over my trousers. Just
look at the state of me and it's my birthday as well.

HANNAH. Is it?

ELLIOTT. It certainly is. I think that calls for a little celebration
myself; an usquebaugh.

HANNAH. What?

ELLIOTT. Whisky. And that looks remarkably like a bottle of
the very stuff to me. You're not going to tell me you're going
to deny a lonely man a birthday drink I'm sure.

He pours two whiskies using the glasses that are there from
HANNAH *and* CHRIS *drinking the night before.* HANNAH
watches.

HANNAH. So how old are you?

ELLIOTT (*he hands her a glass and downs his*). Ah ha. That would
be telling wouldn't it? Are you not joining me?

HANNAH. Is everything there in your wallet?

ELLIOTT. Now you are what I call a perceptive person. How
did you know to ask that?

HANNAH. Is everything there?

ELLIOTT. Yes thank you it is.

HANNAH. Good. If that's what you came for then you can . . . (*She puts her glass down not wanting to drink.*)

ELLIOTT (*interrupts*). That is quite fantastic in fact. It's a long time since I've met anyone quite as observant. What a marvellous quality to have. You don't often meet it believe me. You can obviously see through me because . . . well I must admit the wallet is precious to me. I have been climbing the walls since I lost it . . .

HANNAH (*interrupts*). And now you've found it.

ELLIOTT. You're a straight to the point, no nonsense girl aren't you? I like that. (*Takes out photographs of his two children and gives them to* HANNAH. *She looks at them. He picks up her glass.*) Those are my two: not how they must be looking now. (*He drinks from her glass.*) Patricia's twenty-five now and Roger's nineteen months younger. (HANNAH *gives them back to him.*) Sorry. I'm sorry. Was that your glass?

HANNAH. Looks like it.

ELLIOTT. There's only one way to make amends.

He is about to pour her another drink. She takes the glass from him.

HANNAH. No thanks.

ELLIOTT. A quicky will keep the chill out. It's like a building site in here. I couldn't live here: could you? It's a strange place for Michael to have bought isn't it?

HANNAH. Colin.

ELLIOTT. Colin. Colin.

HANNAH. Have you ever sought help?

ELLIOTT. For what?

HANNAH. Your drinking?

ELLIOTT. That my dear is about the one thing I don't need help with. My wife, my children, school fees, my parents . . .

HANNAH (*interrupts*). I thought you said your daughter was twenty-five.

ELLIOTT. And I'll be paying her school fees until I'm ninety. She's not even grateful. She's turned out an arrogant bitch: that's what a university education does for you. She hasn't got

the time to drop her old man a letter when he sends her a
little something from Hong Kong. I got her a beautiful dress
watch and Roger a camera. At least he let me know it had
arrived. It's their mother's fault: she did everything in her
power to turn them against me. She couldn't handle me. And
always moody. Now you're not a moody sort of girl are you? I
can see that.

HANNAH. I'm thirty.

ELLIOTT. That I do not believe.

HANNAH. Can you just . . .

ELLIOTT (*interrupts*). Are you here on holiday?

HANNAH. How did you get in?

ELLIOTT. Sorry?

HANNAH. You heard.

ELLIOTT. The door was open,

HANNAH. No it wasn't.

ELLIOTT. No you're right. It wasn't.

HANNAH. So how did you get in?

ELLIOTT. My library card: or to be more precise Simon
Mckenna's library card. (*He shows it to her.*)

HANNAH (*approaching the glass parcel*). What's this?

ELLIOTT (*getting up*). Oh that's mine.

HANNAH. Right fine. Do you need a carrier bag?

ELLIOTT. Er . . .

HANNAH. Yes.

ELLIOTT. Yes, I suppose I do.

HANNAH. I'll just get you one. (*She exits.*)

  Enter TUNIS *carrying two carrier bags containing china.*

TUNIS. Who are you?

ELLIOTT. You must be Colin's wife.

  HANNAH *enters with a carrier bag.*

TUNIS. Who is this?

ELLIOTT. How do you do.

HANNAH. Here.

   She gives the carrier bag to ELLIOTT, *who puts the glass parcel in it.*

TUNIS. Who is he?

HANNAH. I don't know.

TUNIS. What's he doing here?

HANNAH. Nothing.

TUNIS. Don't you know him?

HANNAH. No.

TUNIS. Why did you let him in?

HANNAH. I didn't.

TUNIS. How did he get in?

HANNAH. With this library card.

TUNIS. What? He's a tramp. Get out!

ELLIOTT. Yes.

TUNIS. Now!

ELLIOTT. You could take a leaf out of her book: she's a human
   being.

TUNIS. Are you completely deaf? I said Get Out. You're
   trespassing.

ELLIOTT. Yes. That's right I usually am. (*Exit.*)

TUNIS. Why didn't you call the police?

HANNAH. What for?

TUNIS. He stank.

HANNAH. Is that a crime?

TUNIS. I don't believe you two. Who knows what'll happen?
   Next time I come down he'll have moved in.

HANNAH. I shouldn't worry about that.

TUNIS. Colin'd die if he knew you'd let a tramp in here.

HANNAH. He hasn't done any harm. He hasn't stolen anything
   has he?

TUNIS. Oh God. (*She goes and looks outside the front door.*) Could you help me bring these things in? Silly boy left them out here. I thought you said you were going to be in. (HANNAH *goes and picks up the parcels* TUNIS *is referring to.*) They could easily have been stolen sitting out there. . . . I've bought you some china. I suddenly realised you didn't have a single thing to eat off. It's just basic white but it'll do 'til I decide what I want.

HANNAH. Thanks very much.

TUNIS. He's made me feel quite sick. Do you mind if I am honest?

HANNAH. About what?

TUNIS. I wouldn't use that colour on your eyes. Never use a discernible colour.

HANNAH. Oh I forgot. It was just a joke. One of those demonstrators got hold of me. (*She starts to rub it off.*)

TUNIS. No leave it. You look much better. But blue's a mistake. And clean that off will you? (*Referring to the mouth on the television.*) Who did it?

HANNAH. Chris.

TUNIS. She's a bit crazy isn't she? (*Exit through the interior door.*)

Blackout

Scene Six

Saturday evening 6 p.m.

HANNAH *is going through a bag of things she's found on the beach: shells, stones, feathers, seaweed.* CHRIS *has a couple of carrier bags containing things she's got at the shops.*

CHRIS. I don't think it's ever hit me really that the person who's there to support me is me. I don't think I realised the decisions I was making mattered that much. I don't think I knew I was making decisions. I'm wasting myself and I don't know what to do about it. I don't know who the hell I am. I don't know where I belong. I could spend my life lurching from one thing to the next, finding the world more and more intolerable and wanting more and more to escape it and wishing . . .

HANNAH (*interrupts*). When we were at Hull and you used to come out with stuff I used to think you were so clever. Then you seemed to have this wonderful life gadding about Europe or living in Cairo or living in Sydney with a mad sculptor. And whenever you were back here for a while and you were waitressing or something to fill in, you were always bolshy because that's the way you are but you weren't depressed, not like this, because you were always hatching plans to do something else. Why's it all changed?

CHRIS. I've grown up.

HANNAH. That's a pity.

CHRIS. I've finally realised this is my life. I'm not going to be living it soon. I'm living it now. This is it.

HANNAH. I see.

CHRIS. Christ! When I knew Colin he was pathetic. How did he know what he wanted to do? How did he know what was out there that he could do? What made him know that he had to get on with it? They don't even get to be statistics, the rich. They're even above that. I'm loads of statistics. I'm a higher educated non-home owner, an unmarried, childless, self-supporting female, a below-the-national-average wage earner. More than anything I hate being a waitress because that is what I am.

HANNAH. You haven't *always* been a waitress, you're a waitress *now*. The only reason you're one now is you've never stuck at being anything else.

CHRIS. I've never *been* anything. I've just had jobs.

HANNAH. Do something else then.

CHRIS. Like what?

HANNAH. I don't know. Teach . . . There are jobs.

CHRIS. How did you know what you wanted to do?

HANNAH. I didn't. I just fell into it.

CHRIS. You like it though don't you?

HANNAH. Yeah. I love it. I could do something else though. I don't have to teach ceramics for the rest of my life. So long as I've got the time and the space to do what I want with . . .

CHRIS (*interrupts*). What the hell are you meant to be able to do with a geography degree? The only thing I'm qualified to do is flounder. I should have married Colin. At least then by now I'd have credit cards and some kind of lifestyle.

HANNAH. Did he ever ask you?

CHRIS. He would have done sooner or later, or one of them would. If I'd stuck around I'd have ended up marrying one of the Colins of this world or the Christophers or the Richards.

HANNAH. You don't know what you're doing *now*. You haven't *always* not known what you were doing. It's just *now*.

CHRIS. I'm not earning any money.

HANNAH. You are.

CHRIS. Not enough.

HANNAH. Why does everyone always think they've got to earn more money? As if that's going to make them happy. It doesn't make you happy. It just mucks you up.

CHRIS. Don't talk soft. That's so simplistic.

HANNAH. It's not. *That*'s the truth. Money makes you greedy and shortsighted. People don't need half the stuff they think they do. They just get trapped in this spiral of getting more and more and they can't remember what they wanted it all for in the first place. They don't actually use the money to do anything: they just clutter up their lives.

CHRIS. At the rate I'm going, I'm never going to be able to buy anywhere to live. I'm never going to be able to buy a new car. I'm never going to own . . .

HANNAH (*interrupts*). Count yourself lucky. You must be crazy wanting to get tied up in all of that.

CHRIS. Well I do.

HANNAH. Why? What's the point? You don't have to own where you live. There's thousands of ways of being. There are thousands of places people ought to be living in that are sitting empty, going to rack and ruin because we've got it into our heads that the only way to be is like everyone else, scared and timid and pathetic like everyone else: feeling we've got to own things to exist. You don't have to own your own means of transport. You don't have to own your own washing machine. Have you ever thought how ridiculous it is for every single person to have their own washing machine?

CHRIS. Since when has every single person got their own washing machine?

HANNAH. It's the principle.

CHRIS. What principle?

HANNAH. I don't want to own things. How can you share something when you own it? It's a contradiction in terms. Can't you see that? If I owned a house it wouldn't be yours would it?

CHRIS. That's only 'cos you're screwed up about it 'cos your family's loaded.

HANNAH. It's not. I don't believe . . .

CHRIS. Well good for you, I do. Money's not a big problem for me. It's simple in fact. Money is something I'd like to have more of.

HANNAH. My parents aren't that well off and I don't live off their money and I never will.

CHRIS. Look, I'm not like you, I don't want to live in a squat.

HANNAH. It's not a squat. We're in a Housing Association.

CHRIS. Whatever it is it's not what I'm after.

HANNAH. Yes, yes, I know.

CHRIS. She's been on a spending spree hasn't she?

HANNAH. It's revolting stuff isn't it?

CHRIS. Pretty.

HANNAH. I don't see the point in antiques.

CHRIS. Here. (*She pulls a sweater out of a carrier bag.*) I thought it might suit you.

Pause.

Actually I thought it might suit me as well and they're terribly expensive so I nicked two. (*She pulls another one, identical, out of the bag.*)

HANNAH. You're crazy. Weren't you seen?

CHRIS. Who by?

HANNAH. Anyone.

CHRIS. I don't know.

HANNAH. Didn't you look?

CHRIS. Don't be so bloody paranoid. 'Course I looked.

HANNAH. Are you sure?

CHRIS. Sure I'm sure.

HANNAH *puts the sweater on.*

HANNAH. You're going to get caught one of these days you know.

CHRIS. Do you like it?

HANNAH. I thought you'd grown out of shoplifting.

CHRIS. I have. More or less.

HANNAH. You should have done by now. I haven't nicked anything since . . .

CHRIS. You don't have to have it.

HANNAH. No I'll have it. Who's going to have it if I don't? £89.99. Bloody Hell.

CHRIS. Some people would think that was a bargain.

HANNAH. When did you get greedy? You never used to be greedy.

CHRIS. I'm not.

HANNAH. You are. You're always wanting things.

CHRIS. That's just getting even. I didn't expect to not have things, that's the truth of it. I wasn't brought up expecting this. I don't know what I was expecting but . . .

HANNAH (*interrupts*). Anyone who'd pay £89.99 for a sweater needs to have their head examined. I got a beautiful one the other day for £2.50. Much better than this, much better quality.

CHRIS. That one's a freebie.

HANNAH. Well I've been pinching stones off the beach. They're nice aren't they?

CHRIS. What are you going to do with them?

HANNAH. You were right: there has been a drunk in here. I

met him.

CHRIS. What was he like?

HANNAH. *That's* why I don't like being on my own. Whenever I'm on my own I get cornered by some loony who wants to tell me the story of his pesky life.

CHRIS. You should have come shoplifting.

HANNAH. It always happens to me. Always. If there's a loony out there he's going to find me. I met a bloke once who wanted me to help him buy a coffee because he was disabled. Disabled my foot, he was carrying a crash helmet. He'd come on his motor bike. But according to him he was disabled. He wanted me to help him buy a coffee. He wanted to know if I would like one. So I ended up buying us both coffees and talking to him. And you get the whole life story and it's just depressing. It's incomprehensible and you know you're never going to clap eyes on that person again and you've got their sadness and queerness to cart around with you for the rest of time. . . . It's quite a line isn't it? 'Can you help me please I'm disabled.' We're all fucking disabled. If frailty's the bottom line we're all disabled.

Pause.

He smelt too. They always smell.

CHRIS. 'You alright?

HANNAH. Why did he have to find me? Why this bloody human dereliction? It's mad isn't it, not being able to think of anything to do with yourself apart from destroy yourself, drink yourself into the grave?

CHRIS. What was he like?

HANNAH. I have absolutely no idea. He just talked out of a hole in the top of his head. He hated his wife. He'd bought his daughter a dress watch in Hong Kong. She was an arrogant bitch. He'd lost his wallet. Someone's cat had been sick down his front, Ha Ha.

CHRIS. Where did you meet him?

HANNAH. He was here. He wanted his jacket.

CHRIS. The one I chucked out?

HANNAH. Yes. It was all covered in crap. He didn't even notice.

You know the most important thing of all?

CHRIS. What?

HANNAH. Don't go under. Don't go under with anger. Don't go under with fear. Don't give up. It's made me feel a bit . . .

Pause.

CHRIS. It's this place Hannah. It's creepy. It gave me the creeps the moment I walked through the door. You know it did. There's nothing here. It's bound to make you feel weird. It's like spending the weekend in the middle of the road. We might as well have plonked our sleeping bags on the hard shoulder or in the traffic somewhere.

HANNAH. What a shame she's going to fill this room with clutter and it's beautiful the way it is.

CHRIS. You've got to have your creature comforts around you or you just feel funny. You've got to have curtains, hot water, baths, paraphernalia. You need all that stuff or you just feel exposed. Net curtains might have been invented by the English but they did have a point. If you're going to be stuck living in the traffic I reckon you want to be in a large car with smoked glass windows so if you do choose to look out of them they, whoever they may be, won't be able to see that you're looking. So they won't be able to pounce on you for sympathy.

HANNAH. Maybe.

CHRIS. Haven't you ever noticed rich people never get pounced on? They're exempt. Tramps don't ask them for money. They wouldn't dare. They wouldn't dream of lumbering them with the stories of their lives either. It's always girls like you and me who get it.

HANNAH. Maybe.

CHRIS. You'd never find your friend Tunis out on a beach collecting stones and driftwood. She'll either always be in her car or somewhere with curtains and carpets and a hundred locks on the door.

HANNAH. He reeked of alcohol.

CHRIS. Maybe he needs to drink.

HANNAH. Why?

CHRIS. To get himself through things.

HANNAH. He'd get through them anyway.

CHRIS. Yes but he could have a really awful life couldn't he?

HANNAH. He probably has.

CHRIS. Who knows? People who offload their stories on you like that are . . .

HANNAH (*interrupts*). No matter how anxious you are, no matter how obsessed, eventually your mind will wander and you will find yourself thinking about painters or something, fuse boxes, anything, anything and everything and the most inconsequential thing in the world and not your anger or illness or the awfulness of things, not the all-consuming problem at all. And it is that wandering of the mind that keeps the heart and soul from drowning. That's how you learn to live with it, whatever your particular 'it' is. And everybody's got one: no one's exempt. The only thing that is absolutely certain sure is that time is going to pass: you're going to get through it. And you won't think about it again until you're worried about it again. That's the only thing that's sad: we don't seem to notice when we are alright. And we generally are alright. As soon as he hasn't got drink inside him he's going to have to face whatever it is alone and wait for the time to pass. And it will.

CHRIS. Has it churned you up?

HANNAH. A bit: but I've been out on the beach. It's OK. What are we going to do tonight?

CHRIS. Eat.

HANNAH. Is that all?

CHRIS. It's a start.

HANNAH. OK.

CHRIS. If I was going to be a patron saint I suppose I'd have to be patron saint of shoplifting.

HANNAH. I'd be patron saint of swimmers. I'd be patron saint of anything that stays afloat.

Blackout.

Scene Seven

Saturday 9.30 p.m.

CHRIS (*off*). If I can find it again I think that's where we should go.

HANNAH (*off*). Where?

CHRIS (*off*). The club I found

HANNAH (*off*). Can we eat there?

CHRIS (*off*). Yeah.

HANNAH (*off*). Are you sure?

CHRIS (*off*). You must be able to: it's a club.

HANNAH (*off*). Have you got to be a member?

CHRIS (*off*). No.

HANNAH (*off*). Do you know?

CHRIS (*off*). No.

> CHRIS *enters. She is basically wearing the same clothes but has got dressed up a bit. She changes her shoes. She fiddles with her hair and makeup.*

HANNAH (*off*). I don't want to just sit in a restaurant.

CHRIS. No. Right. It'll be good.

HANNAH (*off*). If we can get in.

CHRIS. Oh we'll get in. You don't have to book in these places. I haven't eaten all day. (*She looks at her watch. She puts her coat on.*) It's half past nine . . . Hannah?

HANNAH (*off*). What?

CHRIS. It's half past nine.

HANNAH (*off*). I heard.

CHRIS (*looking for the bottle of whisky*). We didn't finish the whisky did we?

HANNAH (*off*). No.

CHRIS. Where is it? Hannah?

HANNAH (*off*). By the sofa.

CHRIS. It isn't.

HANNAH (*off*). It's somewhere there.

CHRIS. It isn't.

HANNAH (*off*). I don't know.

CHRIS. Your friend Tunis has been in here scoffing it.

HANNAH (*off*). What?

CHRIS. Someone's had it.

HANNAH (*off*). Yes he did.

CHRIS. What?

HANNAH (*off*). The drunk had some.

CHRIS. What?

HANNAH (*off*). What's the problem?

CHRIS. You gave him some of our whisky?

HANNAH (*off*). He took a couple of drinks.

CHRIS. Brilliant.

HANNAH (*off*). What's the matter?

CHRIS. He's nicked the bottle. Aren't you ready yet?

HANNAH (*off*). Just give me five minutes will you?

CHRIS. I'm getting bored.

HANNAH (*off*). Tough.

  PEST *enters through a wall.*

PEST. Did I scare you?

CHRIS. Yes.

PEST. 'You scared of guns? . . . It's not loaded. Did you think it was loaded?

CHRIS. I don't know.

PEST. I'm not going to do anything with it.

CHRIS. Aren't you?

PEST. Did you think it was loaded?

CHRIS. Do you make a habit of plaguing people?

PEST. Dunno.

CHRIS. You do know.

PEST. I don't.

CHRIS. Why do you do it?

PEST. 'S better than doing nothing.

CHRIS. You're so bloody unnecessary.

PEST. So don't ask for it.

CHRIS. I don't ask for it.

PEST. 'Course you do.

CHRIS. How?

PEST. 'Cos you're sitting there.

CHRIS. 'Cos I'm sitting here?

PEST. Yeah.

CHRIS. 'Cos I'm sitting here?

PEST. Yeah.

CHRIS. What's that supposed to mean?

PEST. I don't know: you're just sitting there.

CHRIS. Why shouldn't I sit here?

PEST. I don't know.

CHRIS. Why shouldn't I sit here? What right have you got . . .

PEST (*interrupts*). You shouldn't look so serious.

CHRIS. I don't believe this.

PEST. *Bang*!

He aims at a couple of objects.

Missed. I'm bored now. I hate being bored. I'm always bored. Were you frightened?

CHRIS. Yes.

PEST. Really?

CHRIS. I don't know.

PEST. You weren't just playing?

CHRIS. Were you?

PEST. How come you're frightened when you know it's not for real?

CHRIS. I don't know.

PEST. It's not loaded. There's nothing to be frightened about, so how come you're frightened?

CHRIS. I don't know it's not for real.

PEST. I don't get frightened.

CHRIS. Don't you?

PEST. What is it you're frightened of?

CHRIS. Fear.

PEST. What of?

CHRIS. I'm frightened of fear.

PEST. That's not being frightened. That's just stupid. That's just fucking stupid. *What are you frightened of?*

CHRIS. Don't shout. I hate people shouting.

PEST. You've got to be frightened *of* something. What are you frightened *of?*

CHRIS. *I'm frightened of the unspeakable peril in the day to day.*

PEST. What's that?

CHRIS. Everything.

PEST. That's stupid.

CHRIS. Why don't you make yourself useful?

PEST. I can't.

CHRIS. You could try.

PEST. Nah. I'd feel stupid. I've never made myself useful. Ever.

CHRIS. Is that a fact?

PEST. I really want to shoot something big one day, some big animal. I don't want to kill it especially, I want to shoot it. I want to do the shooting. That's *it* you see. That's what you get off on. It's not the killing or whatever, it's the moment before. It's the moment it's caught, trapped or whatever and anything could happen. That's the moment, not the moment

after 'cos that's when it dies or whatever. But the moment
before's the biggest moment ever . . . It's like when you have
an accident. You know? You go over and over in your head
the time up to it happening don't you? You don't go over it
actually happening 'cos you can't do anything then so there's
no point. You can only play in your head with doing
something before it happens so as to make it not happen.
Yeah? That's when you're at your most alive ever I'm sure, just
before you die. But I couldn't do it with this. This is just for
killing birds and stuff like that.

CHRIS. Why are you telling me this?

PEST. Aren't you interested?

CHRIS. No.

PEST. You're not very friendly are you?

CHRIS. No I'm not.

PEST (*seeing a mark on his jeans*). How did that happen? Shit.
Look. They're ruined. Shit. Look at that. How did that get
there? Look at it. I can't wear these. My Mum'd die if she saw
me out in a filthy pair of jeans like these. How did that
happen? I'll have to change. I can't wear these.

CHRIS. I can't see anything.

PEST. They're filthy. Look. Filthy.

CHRIS. They've got a spot on them.

PEST. I'm not going around like a tramp. I've got standards.
That's not to say I'm a pansy. Not by a long way. I'm not a
pansy boy but I like my jeans clean and I like them pressed.
Can't wear the same jeans more than two days, maximum
three. You can't go out in filthy fucking clothes. You can't
fucking enjoy yourself if you're not comfortable in your gear.
You've got to have standards. I bath every single day. That's
the main reason I live at home. I couldn't afford all the hot
water. And a washing machine. No, you can't enjoy yourself if
you don't feel good.

CHRIS. Give it to me.

PEST. What?

CHRIS. The gun.

PEST. Why?

CHRIS. Give it to me.

PEST. Why?

CHRIS. Go on.

PEST. Ask nicely.

CHRIS. Give me the fucking gun.

PEST. I don't call that nicely.

CHRIS. I need to encounter stupid fucking idiots like you on a train on a Thursday afternoon like I need a hole in the head.

PEST. I'm not stupid. Who are you calling stupid?

CHRIS. I thought you said you were.

PEST. When?

CHRIS. Why did you point it at me?

PEST. 'See what you would do.

CHRIS. Why?

PEST. I didn't do anything. What did I do? I didn't do anything.

CHRIS. Listen. I look up and see a man sitting opposite me with a gun in his hand and he's pointing it at me. What am I supposed to think?

PEST. Think whatever you want. I don't fucking care.

CHRIS. You frightened me.

PEST. Did I?

CHRIS. Yes.

PEST. 'S no big deal.

CHRIS. It is.

PEST. Why? Are you hurt?

CHRIS. No.

PEST. Well then.

CHRIS. You can't go around brandishing a weapon like that . . .

PEST (*interrupts*). It's not a weapon. It was for a laugh.

CHRIS. It wasn't funny.

PEST. No harm done.

CHRIS. How do you know? How do you know what madness there is in this head for you to play around with?

PEST. Bloody Hell. (*He gets up.*) You look alright to me. (*He starts to leave. He stops and turns round. He is holding a water pistol in his hand.*) Lady! (*He shoots himself in the head and exits.*)

HANNAH *enters.*

HANNAH. Come on then.

CHRIS. We'll never get in now.

HANNAH. What?

CHRIS. I've changed my mind. I don't want to . . .

HANNAH (*interrupts*). I haven't. Come on. It'll be good.

HANNAH *exits through the exterior door.* CHRIS *follows.*

Blackout.

Scene Eight

Sunday 11 a.m.

The next morning. TUNIS, HANNAH *and* CHRIS *are in the room.* TUNIS *is in a completely new outfit.* HANNAH *and* CHRIS *are sitting on the sofa. They are both wearing their new sweaters.*

TUNIS. I have no idea how much it will be but it was worth it. Well of course it isn't worth it. No fine is worth it. It's throwing money down the drain but it's a risk I have to take. I like driving fast. I like it almost more than anything else. So it's a price I must be prepared to pay I suppose. Nothing's free is it? Anyway I have only ever been stopped once before so it's quite cheap as indulgences go . . . You're both wearing the same sweater.

CHRIS. I nicked them yesterday.

TUNIS. Nicked them?

CHRIS. Stole them.

TUNIS. Why?

CHRIS. Why not?

TUNIS *takes out her compact and starts doing her lipstick and eye pencil.*

TUNIS. Does Colin know you steal?

CHRIS. Colin thinks I do everything. Colin thinks I live on brown rice and mud, meaningful foot massage, bracing long walks and really enjoying being cold all winter. Colin thinks I'm happy as a clown to have nothing and that having nothing means having no responsibilities, having not a care in the world. Having nothing means not having anything.

HANNAH. Can you see France from here?

TUNIS. I have no idea.

HANNAH. It's only 20 miles or something isn't it? (*She crosses to the window.*) It's such a beautiful day. If you were going to see France I'm sure you'd . . .

TUNIS. Why do you steal?

CHRIS. Why shouldn't I?

TUNIS. I don't.

CHRIS. Don't you?

TUNIS. No.

CHRIS. You don't need to.

TUNIS *puts away her compact and makeup and puts on a spray of perfume. She addresses* HANNAH.

Will you two be going back today?

HANNAH. You *can* see it.

CHRIS. You know the Rockefellers? Well, Grandad Rockefeller, the first Rockefeller, whatever Rockefeller that ever was: he bought everything. He bought all the coal and then all the steel and all the railways. And his son carried on in the same way and his son and his son. So these Rockefellers ended up owning everything. There didn't seem to be much left over for anyone else to buy, not of the big things like industry and the means of production that is. And if anyone had a temporary amnesia and forgot who was in charge and tried to muscle in they got put in hospital or the funny farm or both. These Rockefellers didn't have a strong sense of morality. They probably couldn't even spell 'morality'. And then when they'd got all this money, all this money, and they were sitting on this huge pile of money and they just had more money than anyone else they became philanthropists. They became the most generous human beings on earth and got everyone to turn round and love them after all . . . Well fuck it. Fuck 'em. They wouldn't have got me to love them I can tell you that much . . . And what's Colin made all his money in? Zips. He's made all his money in zips and everyone wants him to come to dinner. 'The Zipman and his lovely lady wife.' He'll probably get knighted. Well people don't want me to come to dinner because I'm bad tempered and they think I'm planning to steal something. And you know what? They're right. As soon soon as I walk through the door I'm thinking about what I'm going to nick. Bar of guest soap, bottle of vodka. I don't care. I'll use it. But you're not allowed to be gloomy are you? You're not allowed to be depressed. It's glum folk like me who are the social liabilities. We might spoil your day. We might not laugh enough at your jokes. We might not appreciate your hospitality enough. We might throw up all over . . .

HANNAH. Leave her alone. It's not her fault.

CHRIS. What's not her fault?

HANNAH. Just stop it.

CHRIS. What's not her fault? She's got brain cells hasn't she? She can talk.

HANNAH. You're getting yourself . .

CHRIS (*interrupts*). She's not a child. She's spent more money in the last 24 hours than you and I have had since God knows when.

HANNAH. Sorry. She's just . . .

CHRIS. I'm not just anything.

TUNIS. Wrong. You're just bloody rude. No wonder no one wants you to come to dinner. You're rude with a warped sense of how to say thank you.

CHRIS. For what?

TUNIS. For Colin's generosity. He doesn't have to be generous you know. He doesn't have to be generous at all.

CHRIS. He's not generous. He's rich. I want to know what makes you so special. How it is that at the age of 19 or 24 or whatever you are your bag is full of credit cards? How it is that you've been into proper jewelry shops and bought real jewelry or at least had it bought for you and you don't look to me like you've done a day's work in your life. You're the enemy, you and Colin and all the other fuckers out there who own more than they know what to do with. I hate you. I hate the rich. You're the only people in the world who get off scot-free. How do you do it? How did you get all that money? How come most of us scrabble around year in year out scared shitless that we're going to go under? *Why did God choose you to be rich?*

TUNIS. I have no idea.

HANNAH. Shut up Chris. You're being ghastly.

CHRIS. I *want* to be. I want to be as unpleasant as possible.

HANNAH. You're succeeding.

TUNIS. This sounds more like envy than hate to me.

CHRIS. What's the difference?

TUNIS. How can you hate me when you don't even know me?

CHRIS. Who says I don't know you? I serve people like you in the restaurant every day.

TUNIS. And what sort of people are people like me?

CHRIS. You're rich. Confident. Indolent. You swan around the world like you own it. The only authority you've got in the world comes from your husband's money.

TUNIS. I wasn't aware that I had any authority.

CHRIS. How come you get what you want then?

TUNIS. I don't get what I want.

CHRIS. Have you any idea how hard it is to keep on the right side of the law let alone the acceptable?

TUNIS. I've never thought about it.

CHRIS. When you're poor you feel everyone's out to get you. You feel everything you do is wrong. You're never in a million years going to get that kind of confidence, the confidence that lets you assume the right to be there. *That* authority.

HANNAH. Damn. France moved.

CHRIS. They said on the radio that in the 21st century the robots will do all the manual work and that will leave people free to do helping sorts of jobs. There'll be 10 per cent keeping a check on the robots and about 15 per cent . . . well I don't remember the percentages. I can't remember what the jobs were. There'll be transport and tourism and the police and the military and the caring people and I can't remember it all but it's a plan for a hundred per cent employment for the future and the main new category will be . . . I can't remember what they said it will actually be called but it's going to account for forty per cent of the workforce and these workers are going to be employed in the helping capacities, servicing people's needs, caring, and all I can say is, 'What are they talking about, the future's here already. It's just no one's getting paid for it yet.' Or if they are getting paid they aren't getting paid enough so they're all on the fiddle like me. But speaking as one of the forty per cent I suppose I should be looking forward to the turn of the century because then I might start getting paid properly.

TUNIS. I thought you were a waitress.

CHRIS. Yes, I'm a waitress so I fiddle the dole. That's what being a waitress means. I'm thirty and I'm still a waitress.

TUNIS. What's wrong with being a waitress?

CHRIS. What's wrong with being a waitress is that it's a shit job with shit money, no shitting pension and zero fucking prospects. That's what's wrong with it.

TUNIS. Why are you a waitress if you're so clever?

CHRIS. Because I never married a zip tycoon.

TUNIS. That's not answering the question.

CHRIS. Unfortunately it is. If you hadn't married Colin you might be a waitress now mightn't you?

TUNIS. I shouldn't think so.

CHRIS. Oh.

TUNIS. I didn't have to marry Colin. I could have married someone else.

CHRIS. What I'm trying to say is . . .

TUNIS. I know what you're trying to say.

CHRIS. I doubt it.

TUNIS. Well I think I do actually. No one's ever said it to me before but I'm not a nitwit. I know I'm lucky. I also know I've never had pretentions to being anything other than what I am. But I don't see any reason at all why I shouldn't want to be happy. And I don't see what my wanting to be happy has to do with you. In fact I cannot imagine how you've managed to make me, personally, feature in your vision of the world and what it's doing to you at all. But never mind.

HANNAH. You're not that lucky. Money's not everything. I wouldn't want to . . .

TUNIS. I've had a bloody awful weekend. I'm worn out with shopping. I bought a mirror yesterday and they smashed it carrying it out to the car. Then I got stopped for speeding. Then I came here with two carrier bags full of china because I realised you didn't have anything to eat off and I found you'd invited a disgusting old tramp in here and defaced the television. And now I have to sit and listen to this! I don't know what your problem is but I can tell you it has nothing to do with me. I'm up to here with problems. I'm buggered if I'm going to take on yours as well.

CHRIS. If you were one half an ounce as insefuckingcure as I have been for a long, long sodding time you might just begin to be able to glimpse at what I'm feeling now. But you never will.

TUNIS. You don't strike me as being insecure.

CHRIS. Is that a fact?

TUNIS. You're not working class. You're not underprivileged. You're not uneducated. I'm not even convinced that you're poor. Why should I feel sorry for you? You're not ill are you? You look well enough to me. You've chosen what you've got haven't you? Things could be different. You could . . .

CHRIS. How the hell do you know? Did you choose to be rich?

Pause.

TUNIS. Yes. Yes I did. Would you have chosen differently if you had had the choice?

HANNAH. I would. I know I don't want to be rich. Look what it does to you?

CHRIS. What do you mean 'generous'? Generous my arse. Colin wouldn't invite his friends to stay here with it in this state, only curiosities like me. There's nothing quite as annihilating as being looked upon as a curiosity. I thought I'd grown out of sleeping on people's floors and being the poor relation. As soon as I walked through the door I had this monumental big *déja vu* of the whole of my life. It feels like every squat I've ever known, every bedsit, every room in someone else's house. When am I going to live somewhere nice? When am I going to feel I'm out of reach of the grim?

TUNIS. Why don't you get a good job?

CHRIS. Why don't you go into the bathroom and stick your head down the lavatory where it belongs?

She exits through the front door.

Pause.

TUNIS. When are you going back?

HANNAH. Sometime this afternoon.

TUNIS. I see.

HANNAH. About five or something.

TUNIS (*looking about her*). At least everything's arriving. That's something.

HANNAH. Yes.

TUNIS. You know Colin is actually very fond of her. He thinks she's made a mess of her life but he likes her. They've known each other for years. She's always made him laugh.

HANNAH. So he'll be upset?

TUNIS. Of course he will. She shouldn't have come to stay if she felt like that should she? Why is she such a mess?

HANNAH. I don't know.

TUNIS. Is her life that awful?

HANNAH. I don't think so.

TUNIS. Why did she have to pick on me?

HANNAH. She could see you spending money like water.

TUNIS. How are you supposed to decorate a place without spending money?

HANNAH. I don't know.

TUNIS. And how does she know I have been spending it like water and what does that mean?

HANNAH. I don't know.

TUNIS. Nobody spends money like water. I don't think stealing's much of a principle. I really don't. And I don't think she's got the monopoly on concern either. The arrogance. She doesn't know the first thing about me.

HANNAH. You're rich.

TUNIS. What on earth does that mean?

HANNAH. You're richer than her.

TUNIS. Yes, exactly. That's what it means. And she's richer, a lot richer than someone who's got nothing at all . . . One of Colin's friends lost eighty six thousand the other night. Eighty six thousand. We were there: we were watching him. That's three, no nearly four times what I've got to spend on this place. When he got up from the table he was looking white but he's not a broken man, not by any means. Who knows, he might have made it up by now? That's rich. How can I take this seriously when it is patently obvious that the only thing Chris wants in life is to get rich herself? And her idea of rich seems to be anyone who is better off than she is.

HANNAH. It isn't the only thing she wants.

TUNIS. I'm not convinced.

HANNAH. She doesn't know what she wants.

TUNIS. And that's my problem?

HANNAH. No.

TUNIS. Why *doesn't* she get a good job?

HANNAH. It isn't that easy.

TUNIS. Oh. What do you do?

HANNAH. I teach ceramics.

TUNIS. Couldn't she do that?

HANNAH. No, actually, she couldn't.

TUNIS. Oh. Surely she can do something. Colin thinks she's very bright. He's always amazed she's still a waitress.

HANNAH. There's nothing wrong with being a waitress.

TUNIS. And what's so wrong with making money?

HANNAH. The concern of people making money is not human welfare but making money, but they tell us that their making money is good for us because that's what's good for people, because prosperity's good for people because it means more people are better off and that, by chance, by accident, by default, but also inevitably and naturally and happily is also about human welfare and betterment and development and fulfilment and progress as well because somehow or other one person's prosperity is another person's prosperity. See?

TUNIS. No.

HANNAH. Exactly. It doesn't make sense. It doesn't add up and we're daft to expect it to. Chris does. I don't. But I also don't care. You see the trouble with all this free enterprise stuff is not everyone wants to operate like that: not everyone wants to be on the make. Some people just want to work. I'm lucky I am working and although it's obvious to me that no one's getting what they deserve I don't want to waste too much of my time worrying about how much I hate the government and privilege and unfairness. I can't honestly see the point.

TUNIS. Chris doesn't want to work. She wants to be well off.

HANNAH. And look what it's doing to her head. Why greed isn't recognised as a major illness of our time is a mystery to me.

TUNIS. Colin is a very generous person.

HANNAH. Did you take the fireplace out?

TUNIS. What fireplace?

HANNAH. This room must have been built with a fireplace.

TUNIS. Do you think so?

HANNAH. Definitely.

TUNIS. No, it's exactly as we found it.

HANNAH. Pity.

TUNIS. Yes, it is isn't it? Do you steal?

HANNAH. No.

TUNIS. I just . . .

HANNAH. I don't want to.

The telephone rings. TUNIS answers it.

TUNIS. Hello . . . It's for you. Chris. (*She hands* HANNAH *the phone.*)

HANNAH. Thanks. (TUNIS *has a look at her purchases.*) Chris? Where are you? . . . What? . . . You lunatic. Where? . . . Can you? . . (*She carries the phone over to the window but the cable won't quite reach.*) It's not long enough . . . Er . . . No . . . Maybe. I don't really know . . . Yes, alright. . . OK. (*She puts the phone down.*)

TUNIS. Has she cooled off?

HANNAH. I think so.

TUNIS *gathers her things together in preparation for leaving.*

TUNIS. You couldn't possibly stay tomorrow as well could you? It's just somebody's coming to give me an estimate . . .

HANNAH. No I can't. Sorry.

TUNIS. They promised they'd get here in the morning.

HANNAH. I'll be at work.

TUNIS. Oh I see. Do make sure you lock up properly won't you? Colin's frantic about the place being squatted.

HANNAH. Of course. Thank you.

TUNIS. Goodbye.

HANNAH. Bye.

TUNIS. Oh and lock the windows.

She exits. HANNAH *goes and looks out of the window and waves.*

Blackout.

Scene Nine

Sunday. Early evening.

CHRIS *and* HANNAH *are leaving. They have their 'overnight' bags packed and are folding up the tent.*

CHRIS. I don't know what I said. I was just enjoying myself. I was being rude to everyone I've wanted to be rude to for years. And I didn't get the sack. It was wonderful. I was being rude to all those rich sods who come into the restaurant and don't leave a tip and all those who moan about everything and don't even notice I exist. I was . . .

HANNAH. And it made no impression on her at all.

CHRIS. 'Course it did. She won't have shown it but it hit the mark.

HANNAH. You upset her.

CHRIS. Because she knows it's true: she's rich and spoilt and doesn't do anything with herself all day long.

HANNAH. 'Nobody does nothing'.

CHRIS. She does.

HANNAH. She's been rushing around all weekend.

CHRIS. Spending money.

HANNAH. You're making yourself ill harbouring all this loathing.

CHRIS. It's good for her to be challenged like that.

HANNAH. She wasn't challenged. The only impression you made on her was of a lunatic with a chip on her shoulder the size of a mountain.

CHRIS. Well, how the hell do you get through to these people?

HANNAH. You stop trying.

Pause.

The rich do not feel guilty for being rich. They're dead proud of it no matter how they've come by their money because everything out there is telling them that what they are doing is right. You're meant to be rich . . . You didn't get within a million miles of her self doubt.

CHRIS. 'Course I did. She just blocked it though. She can't take any of that stuff to heart or her whole universe would crumble.

HANNAH. She thinks you're envious . . . And I think she feels sorry for you.

CHRIS. Bog off.

HANNAH. I do.

CHRIS. I gave her hell.

HANNAH. You made a fool of yourself. It didn't mean anything to her. She doesn't share your world view.

CHRIS. Well I can't help that can I?

HANNAH. You mustn't lash out at people. It'd be different if you lost your temper and had some power like the managing director of some company making millions but you go off your trolley and all you are is a bad tempered waitress. You're in a rage at the state of the world and you're in a rage at your own circumstances and you're not distinguishing between the two.

CHRIS. Because they're the same.

HANNAH. They're not.

CHRIS. You can only say that because you've chosen to live on the sidelines. I don't want to.

Pause.

What did you think of her?

HANNAH. I felt sorry for her.

CHRIS. Did you like her?

HANNAH. Look at yourself Chris. Get a big mirror and look at yourself. You hate yourself. You hate her. But you want her life. You hate her for having the life you want which you despise. Bloody well sort yourself out.

CHRIS. She . . .

HANNAH (*interrupts*). You could have hit thirty married with three children, two red setters, a Colin and a house in Wiltshire and you'd still be pissed off.

CHRIS. What about?

HANNAH. About being married and having three children in Wiltshire.

CHRIS. Don't be stupid.

HANNAH. About everything you're pissed off about now. The News. Global Warming. Other People.

CHRIS. I happen to worry about Global Warming.

HANNAH. And everybody else doesn't? It doesn't matter what you decide to do Chris, so long as you start liking yourself.

CHRIS (*interrupts*). Don't tell me what to do.

HANNAH. If I don't who's going to? Stellios? Hugo's been telling me for weeks you're cracking up and I've been saying you aren't because I know you and I know that's the way you are. But I think he might be right. I'm worried about you.

CHRIS. What does 'cracking up' mean? I'm not very happy. I find it very difficult to be happy. You understand that though, don't you?

HANNAH. Yes but I'm ceasing to find it interesting.

CHRIS. Sorry I've ballsed things up and . . . Don't worry I'm alright. I've got to come to terms with what I'm going to do and I know that if I don't . . . there's two halves to everyone, the hellish and the alright. I've got to get out of the hellish and into the alright. I know I have.

HANNAH. You have Chris or you'll make yourself really ill. But you'll do it. You'll be fine. One thing's got to go right, that's all. And then another will and then all this'll be history.

Everything is now packed up.

Is that it?

CHRIS. Yup.

HANNAH. Come on then.

They make for the exterior door. The television comes on.

CHRIS. Jesus! What did you do?

HANNAH. Nothing.

CHRIS. You must have done something.

HANNAH. I didn't touch it.

CHRIS. God, how creepy.

HANNAH. It's burglar watch.

CHRIS. What?

HANNAH. It's for the burglars to watch.

CHRIS. When?

HANNAH. When they come to nick it.

CHRIS. Bloody hell . . . I'm telling you she was listening. She may not have been showing it but she heard . . . (HANNAH *has exited already*.) You don't listen to that sort of stuff being levelled against you without it penetrating. She's not going to forget that in a hurry. I'm telling you . . .

She exits mid-sentence.

Scene Ten

Tuesday 3 p.m.

The stage is empty. We hear TUNIS *approaching.*

TUNIS (*off, approaching*). I've already had to stay two days longer than I planned. (*Enters.*) The last lot of things I had you deliver the boy left them sitting out there in the hallway. (*She crosses the room and exits through the interior door.*) Anybody could have had them.

Enter LUGGAGE *carrying a piece of furniture.*

I want that in here . . . Are you there? (*Enters.*) There you are. Put that in the . . . Here, I'll show you.

They exit through the interior door.

Yes . . . No. No . . . that's right . . . Oh and take those down to the car. No, not that, the curtains.

LUGGAGE *enters carrying the curtains.* ELLIOTT *enters through the exterior door. He is wearing a morning suit.*

ELLIOTT. Do I look ridiculous?

LUGGAGE. No.

ELLIOTT. I need to know.

LUGGAGE. I don't think so.

ELLIOTT. I don't know if they expect me to be there or not but it's my daughter's wedding and I'm going. I know I could have phoned but . . . I couldn't. Why did she write and tell me if she didn't want me to be there? I'm not going to let her down: I'm not going anywhere near the reception. But I'm going to be at that church. It's a big day for me. Is this too much? Should I just wear a dark suit? I don't know what she'd like. It's not too late. I could change it. I'm not going to put a foot wrong. I couldn't bear to let her down.

LUGGAGE. How you look is not important. Our purpose is not to think much but to love much. Only do that which most inspires you to love.

TUNIS *enters.*

TUNIS. Yes? . . . Can I help you?

ELLIOTT. No. I don't think so.

TUNIS. Have you brought the . . . (*Realising who* ELLIOTT *is.*) This is a private residence. What are you doing here?

ELLIOTT. I thought the other girl was . . .

TUNIS (*interrupts*). She's gone.

ELLIOTT. Has she?

TUNIS. Yes they've both gone and this is my flat and I don't want you in it.

ELLIOTT. Yes.

TUNIS. I want you out. Now. This is the last time anybody stays here who hasn't been invited by me personally. This is absolutely . . .

ELLIOTT (*interrupts*). Just tell me how I look.

TUNIS. What?

ELLIOTT. How do I look?

LUGGAGE. He's going to his daughter's wedding.

TUNIS. I don't believe this.

ELLIOTT. I need to know if I look alright.

TUNIS. Why don't you go and ask somebody?

ELLIOTT. I am asking.

TUNIS. What are you doing here?

ELLIOTT. I'm not doing anything. I'm going now. Just tell me if . . . Should I just wear a dark suit?

TUNIS. I have no idea. I was married in The Dordogne.

ELLIOTT. Do I . . .

TUNIS (*interrupts*). Yes you look absolutely fine. Marvellous. Alright? Now *out.*) And you.

ELLIOT *and* LUGGAGE *move towards the exterior door.*

Come on. Come on.

TUNIS *gets her keys out ready to lock up.* ELLIOTT *and* LUGGAGE *have exited.*

The sooner I can get Colin to put this place on the market the better.

Exit.

Blackout.